# STEM Matters

This resource is your guide to understanding STEM's place within K-12 education, amidst the many meanings and initiatives that swirl around this buzzword in today's schools. Authors Rodger W. Bybee and Patrick L. Brown, who have worked in leadership roles developing curricula and national standards, provide background, explanations, and guidance for demystifying STEM's place in contemporary classrooms and establishing sustainable STEM programs and practices that prepare students for their futures. Chapters are organized around STEM's Purposes, Policies, Programs, and Practices—clarifying what STEM means beyond the acronym, examining the role of educational policies, specifically the Next Generation Science Standards (NGSS), developing coherent school programs, and implementing effective classroom teaching practices. Each STEM discipline is defined alongside concrete recommendations for designing, developing, and implementing instructional materials. Across the sections, the authors focus on small, manageable changes that educators and leaders can develop with their colleagues to formulate and implement. Chapters also include personal educator stories, references to historically significant and contemporary research and examples, recommendations for leadership, and discussion questions. Whether you are a teacher leader, a member of a professional learning community, or a district administrator, this helpful guide should be a key consideration within reform processes, from selecting new programs and developing instructional materials, to providing professional development.

**Rodger W. Bybee** is an Education Consultant, a former K-12 science teacher, and a retired faculty of Carleton College. He was both the executive director of the Center for Science, Mathematics, and Engineering Education at the National Research Council and executive director at the Biological Sciences Curriculum Study. He is also a Writing Team Leader for the Next Generation Science Standards (NGSS).

**Patrick L. Brown** is the Executive Director of STEAM and CTE at Fort Zumwalt School District, and a former science classroom teacher and coordinator.

# Also Available from Routledge Eye on Education
(www.routledge.com/go/routledge-eye-on-education)

**The Explore-Before-Explain Guidebook for Science Education: Creating High Quality Lessons for the Classroom and Professional Learning**
Patrick Brown

**STEM by Design:
Tools and Strategies to Help Students in Grades 4–8 Solve Real-World Problems, 2nd Edition**
Anne Jolly

**Teaching Climate Change for Grades 6–12:
Activating Science Teachers to Take on the Climate Crisis Through NGSS, 2nd Edition**
Kelley T. Lê

**Hydropower Efficiency, Grade 4:
STEM Road Map for Elementary School**
Carla C. Johnson, Janet B. Walton and Erin E. Peters-Burton

**Habitats Local and Far Away, Grade 1:
STEM Road Map for Elementary School**
Carla C. Johnson, Janet B. Walton and Erin E. Peters-Burton

**Habitats in the United States, Grade K:
STEM Road Map for Elementary School**
Carla C. Johnson, Janet B. Walton and Erin E. Peters-Burton

**Culturally Responsive and Sustaining Science Teaching:
Teacher Research and Investigation from Today's Classrooms**
Elaine V. Howes and Jamie Wallace

**STEM Road Map 2.0: A Framework for Integrated STEM Education in the Innovation Age**
Carla C. Johnson, Erin E. Peters-Burton, Tamara J. Moore

**STEM Matters: Your Guide to Educational Purposes, Policies, Programs, and Practices**
Rodger W. Bybee and Patrick L. Brown

# STEM Matters

## Your Guide to Educational Purposes, Policies, Programs, and Practices

Rodger W. Bybee and Patrick L. Brown

NEW YORK AND LONDON

Designed cover image: © Getty Images

First published 2026
by Routledge
605 Third Avenue, New York, NY 10158

and by Routledge
4 Park Square, Milton Park, Abingdon, Oxon, OX14 4RN

*Routledge is an imprint of the Taylor & Francis Group, an informa business*

© 2026 Rodger W. Bybee and Patrick L. Brown

The right of Rodger W. Bybee and Patrick L. Brown to be identified as authors of this work has been asserted in accordance with sections 77 and 78 of the Copyright, Designs and Patents Act 1988.

All rights reserved. No part of this book may be reprinted or reproduced or utilised in any form or by any electronic, mechanical, or other means, now known or hereafter invented, including photocopying and recording, or in any information storage or retrieval system, without permission in writing from the publishers.

For Product Safety Concerns and Information please contact our EU representative GPSR@taylorandfrancis.com. Taylor & Francis Verlag GmbH, Kaufingerstraße 24, 80331 München, Germany.

*Trademark notice*: Product or corporate names may be trademarks or registered trademarks, and are used only for identification and explanation without intent to infringe.

ISBN: 978-1-041-02225-1 (hbk)
ISBN: 978-1-041-02186-5 (pbk)
ISBN: 978-1-003-61820-1 (ebk)

DOI: 10.4324/9781003618201

Typeset in Palatino
by SPi Technologies India Pvt Ltd (Straive)

# Contents

*Meet the Authors* — vii
*Preface* — x
*Acknowledgements* — xii

1  STEM Matters: An Introduction — 1

**PART I**
**STEM EDUCATION— REALITIES, POSSIBILITIES, AND PRIORITIES** — 13

2  Realities: STEM Is Here; and So Are Science Standards — 15

3  Possibilities: Thinking Differently About STEM Education — 22

4  Priorities: Reasonable and Prudent Recommendations for STEM Education — 28

**PART II**
**INTRODUCING FOUNDATIONS FOR THE STEM DISCIPLINES** — 35

5  Science: A Way of Explaining Phenomena in the World — 37

6  Technology: A Way of Adapting by Humans — 45

7  Engineering: A Way of Designing Solutions for Human Problems — 52

8  Mathematics: A Way of Quantifying and Expressing Relationships — 58

**PART III**
**EXPLORING PURPOSES, POLICIES, AND PERSPECTIVES FOR STEM PROGRAMS AND PRACTICES FOR STEM EDUCATION** — 63

9  The Purposes of Education, Including STEM — 65

10  Policies for STEM Education, Including Standards — 76

| 11 | STEM Programs, Including Curriculum and Assessment | 84 |
|---|---|---|
| 12 | STEM Practices: Using Effective Instructional Sequences | 95 |

**PART IV**
**CULTIVATING STEM TEACHER EXPERTISE** — **105**

| 13 | Centering Efforts on the Instructional Core | 107 |
|---|---|---|
| 14 | Beginning with a Manageable Unit | 115 |
| 15 | Enhancing Learning: Essential Practices and Impactful Instructional Sequences | 128 |

**PART V**
**DEVELOPING DISTRICT-WIDE STEM PROGRAMS AND PRACTICES** — **137**

| 16 | Establishing a Plan for Change | 139 |
|---|---|---|
| 17 | Evaluating STEM Instructional Materials and Resources | 144 |
| 18 | Curriculum-Based Professional Learning | 153 |
| 19 | Our Vision for Your Guidance and Leadership in STEM Education | 162 |

# Meet the Authors

**Rodger W. Bybee**
This introduction summarizes my professional experiences and several influences and insights from my career. As you will see, my journey did not follow a single, direct path. As a first-generation college student, my original vision was to become a teacher for biology or Earth Science. With experiences teaching those disciplines, my vision expanded to one of becoming a college or university professor of science education. Subsequently, I sought experience, research, and graduate study that contributed to that goal. As my career progressed, I had diverse opportunities that contributed to a broad understanding of education and a variety of leadership experiences.

In the late 1960s, I began teaching ninth-grade Earth Science and high school biology in the Greeley, Colorado, public schools and later at the Laboratory School, University of Northern Colorado (UNC). My first experience with excellent curriculum materials was when I used the Earth Science Curriculum Project (ESCP), Biological Sciences Curriculum Study (BSCS), and several elementary school programs—including the Science Curriculum Improvement Study (SCIS). In my position at the University of Northern Colorado's Laboratory School, I had undergraduate observers in my classroom on a daily basis.

My next milestone was graduate study at New York University. Beyond the usual course work, during my second year, I worked in an elementary school in Manhattan (PS-33), collaborating with teachers to improve their curriculum and instruction.

My next career opportunity included 15 years of teaching in the education department at Carleton College, a liberal arts college in Northfield, Minnesota. Being a faculty member opened a range of opportunities—for example, teaching a course on sustainable society and broadening and deepening my understanding of educational psychology, philosophy, and science and technology policy.

In 1985, I joined BSCS as associate director. The next decade entailed writing proposals and assuming leadership for designing and developing innovative school science programs for elementary, middle, and high school students and undergraduate nonmajors.

In the early 1990s, I worked on national standards and chaired the science content group for this initiative at the National Research Council (NRC) in Washington, D.C. *The National Science Education Standards* (NSES) were released in late 1995 (with a 1996 copyright). Shortly before the release, I joined the NRC as executive director of the Center for Science, Mathematics, and Engineering Education (CSMEE). This role introduced me to leadership at the national level through interactions with federal agencies, congressional committees, and the executive branch.

I returned to BSCS as executive director in 2000 and remained there until I retired in 2007. In the early years of the 21st century I advised on science content for the National Assessment of Educational Progress (NAEP), Trends in Math Science Study (TIMSS), and chaired the science expert group for the 2006 OECD Program for International Student Assessment (PISA). Since retirement I have continued publishing and working as a consultant. For example, I worked on *A Framework for K-12 Science Education* (NRC 2012) and the *Next Generation Science Standards* (NGSS) Lead States (2013).

Throughout my career, I have published articles in refereed journals such as the *Journal of Research in Science Teaching, Science Education*, the *International Journal of Science Education, American Biology Teacher*, and *Educational Leadership*.

Working with mentors taught me about facing challenges, developing standards, and providing leadership. My work broadened from its original exclusive perspective on science education to include technology, engineering, and mathematics, i.e., STEM, and I benefitted from perspectives that included teaching at the elementary, middle, and high school levels, as well as at the undergraduate and graduate levels. My understanding of the history of curriculum development, national policy, and psychology and philosophy have influenced my view of science and STEM education. My background has offered me broad and deep perspectives of educational leadership as the aims of science/STEM education shift with changing social and political priorities. My journey as a science educator has included time as a classroom teacher and an educational leader. I had wonderful mentors from whom I learned about both excellent teaching and effective leadership.

**Patrick L. Brown**

As a coauthor of this book, you might wonder how my experiences have shaped its content. My journey has been diverse and enriching, spanning roles as a classroom teacher, educator in various prospective teacher development programs, leader in professional learning development and implementation, and currently, as the Executive Director of STEAM and CTE for the Fort Zumwalt School District in St. Charles, MO.

My passion for ensuring students are success-ready in K-12 education and beyond has driven my work. In my role as Executive Director, I collaborate closely with teachers to develop STEAM and Career and Technical Education curricula that equip students with the knowledge and skills they need for today's and tomorrow's workforce. Together, we create sequences of courses, i.e., "pathways," that build on each other, enhancing students' understanding and problem-solving abilities. I stay attuned to regional and national occupational trends, preparing teachers to approach instruction from a more pedagogical perspective, always with students' needs at the forefront.

My previous roles as a science coordinator and classroom teacher have deeply influenced my approach to developing STEAM and CTE programs. I have focused on essential lesson components, bundling them to create impactful curricula. My extensive writing on sequencing science lessons through my National Science Teaching Association (NSTA) books series *Instructional Sequence Matters* reflects my dedication to translating effective teaching practices into broader educational impacts. My work comes from both research and practitioner mindsets. I have published articles in research journals such as *Science Education*, the *International Journal of Science Education*, and the *Journal of Research in Science Teaching*, and articles for teachers in *Science and Children*, *Science Scope*, and *The Science Teacher*.

Working as a classroom teacher, developing curriculum, and creating programs for students has taught me about the challenges many educators face. I have learned in my transition to a leadership role that our expectations of teachers are higher than ever and that we must balance how we honor educators' talents and gifts with innovative ways to better prepare students for the real world. My hope is that my work enables students to leave school with the emerging skills and knowledge to make informed decisions in their lives, be competitive in postsecondary education, and be the best candidates for professions they aspire to through the more intentional preparation of teachers.

# Preface

Since its origin in the 1990s the acronym STEM has developed a broad use within the educational community. As a general reference to science, technology, engineering, and mathematics, the slogan serves as a reference and rallying representation for the disciplines and array of educational activities, initiatives, competitions, and careers. However, in time a slogan may be criticized for its lack of definitional clarity and confusion when applied to practical situations. Statements such as "I have STEM activities" or "We participated in a STEM competition" beg questions of what, specifically, are the educational goals relative to the four STEM disciplines?

We propose that the slogan STEM now faces the challenge of progressing from a popular slogan to a clear and coherent component of the educational system. If STEM matters, and we think it does, what are the purposes of STEM education? What are appropriate policies for STEM programs and teaching practices?

This book uses the domains of Purposes, Policies, Programs, and Practices as sections providing background, explanations, and guidance for leaders initiating changes that address the challenge of advancing STEM from a slogan to a substantive and sustainable component of education.

This book begins with discussions of current realities, possibilities, and priorities of STEM if it is to attain a prominent place in education. The chapters proceed with descriptions of STEM disciplines, discussions of educations' purposes, the influence of policies, and practical actions for programs, and practices.

With the aim of establishing STEM as an important innovation in education, this book:

- Helps educational leaders increase their understanding of the STEM disciplines,
- Makes connections between contemporary state standards and STEM programs,
- Clarifies current themes in education—citizenship, college, and careers,
- Recognizes the contributions of STEM to personal and societal challenges,

- ♦ Describes reasonable and prudent processes for reform within the educational system,
- ♦ Addresses the need for curriculum-based professional learning for teachers, and
- ♦ Provides helpful information and experiences as a resource for those guiding STEM education.

To conclude, the late 1950s and 1960s STEM community responded to critical social issues and educational priorities to produce *Sputnik*-spurred reforms. Now, it is time for guidance and leadership reforms that include the creation of high-quality integrated, instructional materials and effective teaching strategies that address the grand challenges of society with substantive and sustainable instructional programs and practices. In short, it is time to move beyond slogans and make STEM education a reality for all students.

Rodger W. Bybee<br>
Patrick L. Brown<br>
July 2025

# Acknowledgements

Support for this book begins with our families and extends to colleagues, friends, reviewers, and Routledge's staff.

Rodger expresses his appreciation to his wife Kathryn Bybee for her understanding, advice, and support. I extend my gratitude to close colleagues who recognize the value of this book: Harold Pratt, Herb Brunkhorst, James Short, and Janet Carlson.

Pat dedicates his work on this book to Dr. Bernard DuBray and Jen Waters, whose commitment to making STEAM a reality for K-12 students has been an inspiration. I am also deeply grateful to the Fort Zumwalt School District for its enthusiastic support of STEAM initiatives. A special thank you to my family—my wife, Cathy Brown, and our children, Lua and Finn—for their constant love and encouragement.

Routledge had the proposal for this book reviewed by five experienced and insightful individuals. The recommendations by Nickalas Collins, Kansas City Public Schools; Topher Miller, Chartwell School; Tonya Woolfolk, Houston County School District; Anne Farley Schoeffler, Seton Catholic School; and Ilana Cyna, Leo Baeck Day School did, without exception, improve the final manuscript.

From the earliest discussions, Julia Dolinger, the Commissioning Editor for Routledge, expressed support and understanding. Thank you Julia. Other members of the Routledge team include Poppy Knight and Sofia Cohen.

Lyn Massey did an excellent job of entering and formatting the manuscript. We thank Lyn for presenting the project in superb form.

# 1

# STEM Matters

## An Introduction

The acronym STEM, representing science, technology, engineering and mathematics, is a very popular slogan in American education. Unfortunately, the acronym also has an extraordinary variety of meaning and initiatives. This situation presents the educational community with several fundamental questions:

- What is STEM education?
- Why does STEM education matter?
- Do standards matter in STEM education?
- Does STEM have a place and possible long-term future in education?

We begin by looking at the book's title—*STEM Matters: Your Guide to Educational Purposes, Policies, Programs and Practices.*

The term STEM Matters refers to both the acronym's importance and the various subjects, themes and ideas. "Your Guide" suggest leadership, a sub-theme that pervades the book. However, discussions of leadership remain in the background of explanations while it certainly may be in the foreground for those with leadership responsibilities.

Finally, the reference to "Educational Purposes, Policies, Programs and Practices" signals significant perspectives and the book's progress from major goals to practical strategies for teaching.

Before progressing too far, we briefly address the first question.

## What Is STEM Education?

How would you answer the question that leads this section? Can you effectively define STEM education? As you think about an answer, what do you consider? Do you think of the acronym's disciplines in different educational programs? Or, perhaps, in robotic competitions, conference titles, summer workshops, and other examples? While the acronym STEM is immensely popular in education, the meanings also have large variations.

The education community must move beyond STEM as a slogan and establish a clear and sustainable definition for STEM as it applies to school programs and teaching practices. To this end, the book aims to: (1) clarify contemporary rationale for STEM education, (2) provide guidance for STEM programs and practices, (3) clarify different educational domains for STEM – i.e., purposes, policies, programs, and practices, and (4) identify contexts for teaching and learning.

STEM had its origins in the 1990s at the National Science Foundation (NFS) and has been used as a generic label for any event, policy, program, or practice that involves one or several of the STEM disciplines. We think it is fair to say that the NSF personnel simply needed an acronym for a range of disciplines for which they had contracts, grants, and other projects. Their intention was not to propose a title for education programs; for example, the education community has embraced a slogan without really taking the time to clarify what the term might mean when applied beyond a general label. When most individuals use the term STEM, they mean whatever they meant in the past. So, STEM is usually interpreted to mean science or math and seldom a coordination of the four disciplines in a program.

If STEM education is going to advance beyond a slogan, educators will have to be clear about what the acronym actually means for educational purposes, policies, programs, and practices. The following discussion presents several things that STEM might refer to in contemporary education. First, it may be a recognition of science, and by their close association, technology engineering, and mathematics in school programs.

Second, STEM may mean an increased emphasis of technology in school programs. With reference to technology, there are very few other things that influence our everyday existence more and about which citizens know less. It is time to change this situation. We are referring to a perspective and education programs larger than Information and Communication Technology (ICT). ICT is, of course, part of technology programs.

Third, STEM could mean increasing the recognition of engineering in K-12 education. Engineering is directly involved in problem solving and innovation, two popular themes (Lichtenberg, Woock, & Wright, 2008). Engineering has some presence in our schools, but certainly not the amount consistent with its careers and contributions to society. If the nation is truly interested in innovation, recognizing the T and E in STEM would certainly be worth increased recognition.(Katehi, Pearson, & Feder, 2009).

Fourth, all STEM disciplines present opportunities for stressing 21$^{st}$-century workforce skills. Students can develop skills such as adaptability, complex communication, social skills, nonroutine problem solving, self-management/self-development, and systems think (NRC, 2010). In STEM programs, student investigations and projects present the time and opportunity for teachers to help students develop these skills.

Fifth, STEM could mean an integrated curricular approach to studying grand challenges of our era. We refer to challenges such as energy efficiency, resource use, environmental quality, hazard mitigation, and personal and social health. The competencies that citizens need in order to understand and address issues such as these are clearly related to the STEM disciplines.

Now is the time to move beyond the slogan and make STEM literacy for all students an educational priority. The public may be ready for such a reform (Johnson, Richkind, & Ott, 2010).

In this book we propose broad purposes for STEM education. This point of view centers on goals. The larger, national sense of advancing STEM education should focus on three aims:

- Achieving higher levels of STEM literacy for all citizens,
- Developing a deep technical workforce—one that meets 21st-century needs, and
- Attaining an advanced research and development workforce with diverse individuals in the professions.

To be more specific, STEM literacy includes the conceptual understandings and procedural skills and abilities needed for all individuals to address STEM-related personal, social, and global issues. For example, STEM education would include basic concepts and processes of STEM disciplines and include appropriate content from state standards. Education for STEM literacy would address the following goals:

- Acquire scientific, technological, engineering, and mathematical knowledge and use that knowledge to competently identify issues, acquire new knowledge, and apply the knowledge to STEM-related issues.
- Understand the characteristic features of STEM disciplines as forms of human endeavors that include the processes of inquiry, design, and analysis.

♦ Recognize how STEM disciplines shape our material, intellectual, and cultural world.
♦ Engage in STEM-related issues and with the ideas of science, technology, engineering, and mathematics as concerned, affective, and constructive citizens.

Translating this description of STEM literacy into school programs and instructional practices requires a way of organizing education so the respective disciplines can be integrated and instructional materials designed, developed, and implemented. Educators must confront and resolve a number of challenges if they are to advance STEM literacy.

One of the most significant challenges centers on introducing STEM-related contemporary issues. Developing the competencies to address the issues students will confront as citizens is essential. Addressing this challenge requires an educational approach that first places life situations and global issues and uses the four disciplines of STEM to understand and address the problems. This has been referred to as context-based science education (Fensham, 2009) and could easily be represented as context-based STEM and implies using problem-based, place-based, or project-based approaches to instructional materials.

## Perspectives that Matter for STEM Education

The book's subtitle—"Your Guide to Educational Purposes, Policies, Programs and Practices" refers to domains within a framework for describing STEM initiatives. The book's major sections progress from *purposes*, e.g., aims and goals; to *policies*, more specific statements such as state standards and districts' curriculum framework; to *programs*, which are the actual instructional materials for STEM education; and, finally, to *practices*, the specific strategies, sequences, and actions for teaching STEM.

You will find it useful to recognize these different perspectives in your work. The perspectives may be expressed by individuals, groups, or organizations within the STEM education community. Some, for example, express views of goals while others state public policies, concerns about school curricula and effective teaching strategies.

The different perspectives express individuals' or groups' professional orientation and concerns. STEM teachers, for example, have understandable classroom and teaching concerns while some educators have policy views as they describe major reforms and the implications for states, districts, schools, and classrooms.

We provide introductory explanations of educational purposes, policies, programs, and practices in the following paragraphs.

*The Purposes of STEM Education.* STEM educators have expressed many aims, goals, and objectives in documents, such as professional reports, articles, school syllabi, and descriptions of competitions. For this perspective we use the term "purposes" as it refers to universal aims and goals of what K-12 STEM education should achieve. Achieving STEM literacy is a statement of purposes. The strength of a purpose statement lies in its widespread acceptance and general agreement within the STEM education community. One weakness lies within the statement's ambiguity concerning specific situations in STEM education. For example, what does the goal of achieving STEM literacy mean for: an elementary school teacher, high school chemistry teacher, a teacher educator, policy maker, or a curriculum developer? The answers, of course, vary for different situations – hence the need for more concrete statements and the translation of the purpose statements for various components of the STEM education community. These more specific statements, based on purposes, introduce the policies.

*Policies for STEM Education.* Policy statements are concrete translations of the purposes for various aspects within the STEM education community. Documents that give direction and guidance, but are not actual programs for courses or teaching, serve as policies. Examples of policy documents include designs for a fifth grade STEM unit, an outline for a high school integrated STEM course, district syllabi for K-12 STEM, and a framework for STEM education.

Likewise, college or university requirements for undergraduate teacher education and state frameworks for assessing STEM disciplines also fall into the category of policies. At the national level, examples of policy documents include the *Next Generation Science Standards* (NGSSLead States, 2013) and *The Technology and Engineering Literacy Framework for the 2014 National Assessment of Educational Progress* (NAGB, 2013), *Common Core State Standards for ELA and Math* (2010), and *Principles and Standards for School Mathematics* (NCTM, 2000).

*Programs for STEM Education.* Programs, for example, include the actual curriculum materials, textbooks, and courseware based on the policies. Major categories of programs include instructional materials, assessments, teacher education courses, and professional development workshops. Programs are unique to grade levels, disciplines, and aspects of STEM education, such as robotic competitions or a middle school integrated STEM curriculum.

STEM programs may be developed by organizations and marketed commercially, or they may be developed by local school districts. Who develops the materials is not the defining characteristic; the fact that schools, colleges, state agencies, and national organizations have programs aligned with policies such as state standards is the important feature of this aspect of STEM education.

*Practices in STEM Education.* Practices refers to the specific methods and strategies of teaching STEM in schools, colleges, or universities. (Note: We have tried to be clear when discussing teaching practices and the science, technology, and engineering practices of contemporary standards.) The strategies of STEM education include the personal interactions between teachers and students and among students, as well as the roles and uses of assessment, educational technologies, laboratories, and other methods for teaching STEM. In the perspectives described here, implementing new classroom strategies implies they would be consistent with polices, programs and would be designed to achieve purposes of STEM literacy, for example.

Improving the practices of teaching STEM centers on the most individual, unique, and fundamental aspect of the "map." STEM educators can propose new goals, reform state standards, syllabi, and scope and sequence charts, and they can develop new curriculum materials, but the critical aspect of any reform is improving teaching and enhancing learning in STEM classrooms.

Recognizing these perspectives in STEM education is relatively new. As you will see, for decades science educators have recognized the importance of goals, curriculum programs and classroom practices, less attention has been directed to questions of policy. Typical discussions have been framed by challenges of topics, such as "theory to practice." The purposes, policies, programs, and practices (the 4Ps) of STEM education exist interdependently.

Although one may be tempted to think of the 4Ps as a sequence of stages such that the ideal would begin with purpose and develop policies followed by programs and practices, history indicates that reforms in education do not reflect this ideal. Different reforms of STEM education have been initiated and have emphasized different elements of the 4Ps.

One can view discussions, articles, and reports on STEM education in at least four connected and interconnected prospectives: purposes, policies, programs, and practices. Each perspective has advocates and audiences, problems and solutions, and roles and responsibilities in STEM education. The challenge of leaders is to recognize these perspectives as they all have their place in STEM education.

In the STEM education community, the variety of reports, standards, and studies presents what may be a confusing array of destinations and proposed direction. A simple map is quire helpful for locating and clarifying different efforts in the geography of contemporary STEM education (see Table 1.1).

Because there are different perspectives, the "summary" will help you recognize where you are and where others are "coming from." Such a map

**TABLE 1.1** A Summary of Perspectives on Initiatives for Reform in STEM Education

| **Purposes** |
|---|
| Purpose statements include aims, goals, and rationales. These statements tend to be universal, abstract, and apply to all components of STEM education. Although it presents elements of both purpose and policy, *A Framework for K-12 Science Education: Practices, Crosscutting Concepts and Core Ideas* (NRC, 2012) has served as a purpose in this era of standards-based reform. "Achieving STEM Literacy for all students" is a specific purpose statement. |
| **Policies** |
| Policies are more specific statements of purposes. Standards, benchmarks, syllabi, frameworks, and strategic plans based on the defined purposes are examples of state and local policies for STEM. Policy statements are concrete translations of the purpose and apply to specific components such as K-12 instructional materials and assessments. The *Next Generation Science Standards* (NGSS Lead States, 2013) is the policy statement most applicable to this discussion. |
| **Programs** |
| Programs are the actual instructional materials used in states, schools, and classrooms. Programs are unique to disciplines, K-12 grades, and levels in the education system. Curriculum materials for K-12 STEM and state assessments are different examples of programs. Programs are a translation of policies to the unique requirements of materials usable by practitioners. |
| **Practices** |
| Practices refer to the specific actions of educators as they implement the program. Classroom teaching of STEM is an example. Practices are the most unique and fundamental level of translating the purposes of STEM education to classrooms. |

will assist you in identifying the location, means of movement, and the direction and difficulties of navigation in the STEM education system.

## An Overview of the Book

Numerous reports support the need for leadership and recommendations relative to education "basis" as educators consider responses to demands for reform. Those demands may be based on national priorities, new state standards, or local issues for example. Considerations for change should be grounded in education and built on educators' current knowledge, abilities, and experiences. Briefly, the book's purpose is to help educators develop deeper understanding of basic educational components as they address the reform of school programs and teaching practices.

The educational community has responded to the need for change with a variety of initiatives under the slogan STEM. There is a contemporary need for a broader and more coordinated approach for K-12 education in science, technology, engineering and mathematics (STEM). This book uses a model that identifies four educational domains helpful for describing change and defining STEM education. Those domains are purposes, policies, programs, and practices.

The book uses the four domains as the orientation for realizing the general educational *purposes*, specific *policies*, and ultimately the concrete school *programs* and classroom *practices*.

The book's chapters are associated with fundamental decisions leaders must make about what should be taught that will contribute to students' preparation for college, careers, and life as productive adult citizens. The perspectives discussed are historical, philosophical, and psychological, but always emphasizing practical issues of leadership for professionals' teaching and students' learning. As leaders in the STEM education community search for new directions, they rely on their knowledge, values and abilities to make sensible and appropriate decisions for their school programs, teaching practices, and especially the unique qualities and needs of their colleagues and students.

The benefits of this book are both fundamental and varied. Readers will:

- Realize connections between the disciplines of STEM education.
- Review the purposes of STEM education and their influence on policies, programs, and practices.
- Be introduced to perspectives for STEM literacy.
- Gain knowledge and insights about two generations of national standards for STEM education.
- Increase their knowledge of designing, developing, and implementing curriculum materials.
- Learn about an effective instructional model and its research foundation.

Each chapter includes an introduction intended to engage the reader. The introduction is followed by personal experiences that explore ideas about the chapter's topics. This is followed by sections on the chapter's topic. This discussion includes references to historically significant reports, books, etc., as well as contemporary research and examples. The chapters conclude with recommendations for leadership and discussion questions. Table 1.2 presents summaries of the book's chapters.

**TABLE 1.2** Organization of *STEM Matters*

| |
|---|
| **Chapter 1: STEM Matters: An Introduction** |
| **Part I: STEM Education – Realities, Possibilities, and Priorities** |
| **Chapter 2: Realities: STEM Is Here; And So Are Science Standards**<br>This chapter introduces several issues associated with both contemporary STEM education and conventional standards-based science education. STEM needs to progress beyond a slogan and varied expressions and science education needs to recognize a variety of contemporary issues. |
| **Chapter 3: Possibilities: Thinking Differently About STEM Education**<br>This chapter presents possible changes to offset challenges to both STEM and state standards for science education. STEM programs can address societal issues not in national, state, and local standards, for example. |
| **Chapter 4: Priorities: Reasonable and Prudent Recommendations for STEM Education**<br>This chapter introduces three goals for STEM education: STEM literacy for citizens, STEM skills and abilities for the 21st-century workforce and STEM careers. This chapter recommends introducing and clarifying the STEM disciplines, recognizing meaningful topics of study for students, designing and developing instructional materials, and using curriculum-based approaches for teachers' professional learning. A proposed reasonable and prudent change of program and practice is a unit of instruction. |
| **Part II: Introducing The STEM Disciplines** |
| **Chapter 5: Science: A Way Of Explaining Phenomena in the World**<br>Science begins with questions and proceeds with gathering evidence and the use of the evidence to propose answers to the questions. Scientific explanations can be broader than answers to questions. They may develop models, identify laws, and construct theories – all based on empirical evidence. |
| **Chapter 6: Technology: A Way of Adapting by Humans**<br>Technological innovations originate with human wants and needs and may include information, communication, transportation, and associated artifacts. Technological innovations must be designed within natural and human constraints. |
| **Chapter 7: Engineering: A Way of Designing Solutions for Human Problems**<br>Engineering is a body of knowledge and processes for solving problems. It is closely related to technology and can be summarized as "design under constraint." Constraints include natural laws and time, money, and the quality of proposed solutions. |

*(Continued)*

**TABLE 1.2** (Continued)

| |
|---|
| **Chapter 8: Mathematics: A Way of Quantifying and Expressing Relationships**<br>Mathematics includes the study of patterns and relationships among quantities, numbers, and space. The possible relationships can be among abstractions without real-world connections. Mathematics may also address experiences and phenomena and applications in the real world. Mathematics has useful applications in a broad complex of disciplines. |
| **Part III: Purposes, Policies, and Perspectives for STEM Programs and Practices** |
| **Chapter 9: The Purposes of Education, Including STEM**<br>This chapter briefly review several historical statements about the purposes of education. The priorities proposed for STEM literacy—contexts, competencies, citizenship—do have historical precedent. |
| **Chapter 10: Policies for STEM Education, Including Standards**<br>This chapter presents an essential question, one that identifies guiding principles for STEM education in the 21st century: What knowledge, values, skills, and sensibilities are essential for STEM literate citizenship in the 21st century? The chapter elaborates on the question by addressing STEM literacy, important policies for a deep technical workforce, and STEM careers. |
| **Chapter 11: STEM Programs, Including Curriculum and Assessments**<br>Using contemporary principles of learning, this chapter addresses the issue of incorporating meaningful contexts in school programs. |
| **Part IV: Cultivating STEM Teacher Expertise** |
| **Chapter 12: STEM Practices: Using Effective Instructional Sequences**<br>This chapter explores various methods for sequencing STEM instructional activities to promote student understanding and sensemaking. The chapter synthesizes contemporary learning theories and classroom instructional models to clarify the connection between effective instructional design and enhanced STEM education. It emphasizes that improving teaching practices and structuring coherent instructional sequences are fundamental to optimizing learning outcomes in STEM classrooms. |
| **Chapter 13: Centering Efforts on the Instructional Core**<br>This chapter presents a cohesive framework for advancing STEM education by aligning modern standards, curriculum programs, and professional learning—three essential "legs" of the instructional core. It emphasizes the importance of balance and integration among these elements to support systemic, sustainable STEM teaching and learning improvement. |
| **Chapter 14: Beginning with a Manageable Unit**<br>This chapter offers a structured approach to launching STEM instruction using the Understanding by Design (UbD) framework. It focuses on backward planning, integration of learning goals, and a severe weather and climate change example. It emphasizes starting small with coherent instructional sequences that are feasible, standards-aligned, and grounded in real-world phenomena. |

*(Continued)*

**TABLE 1.2** (Continued)

| |
|---|
| **Chapter 15: Enhancing Learning: Essential Practices and Impactful Instructional Sequences**.<br>Building on Chapter 14, this chapter highlights five key instructional considerations—activating student ideas, evidence-based claims, enhancement activities, metacognition, and instructional sequencing—to design meaningful and engaging STEM learning experiences grounded in how students learn best. |
| **Part V: Action Plans and Process** |
| **Chapter 16: Establishing a Plan for Change**<br>This chapter outlines a cost–risk–benefit framework for STEM leaders evaluating new instructional resources and emphasizes aligning curriculum selection with learning outcomes, instructional goals, and implementation feasibility. It offers practical tools for small-scale curriculum evaluation and guides teams in selecting resources that support integrated and effective STEM learning. |
| **Chapter 17: Evaluating STEM Instructional Materials and Resources**<br>This chapter provides educators with evaluation criteria for STEM resources, focusing on alignment with learning goals, instructional design, assessment, STEM integration, and classroom practicality. It distinguishes among STEM program models—activity-based, interdisciplinary, and transdisciplinary—and guides users in selecting materials that foster deep, transferable learning. |
| **Chapter 18: Curriculum-Based Professional Learning**<br>Framing professional learning as a three-step process (engage, analyze, apply), this chapter demonstrates how teachers can experience, reflect on, and apply inquiry-based STEM instruction. It underscores the importance of learner-centered, standards-aligned professional learning that mirrors high-quality STEM teaching and fosters sustainable instructional change. |
| **Chapter 19: Our Vision for Your Guidance and Leadership in STEM Education**<br>This chapter reviews the book's overarching themes and presents a forward-looking vision for STEM in American education. The chapter clarifies the crucial roles of guidance and leadership in the STEM context, providing insights into effective leadership principles and strategic priorities for reform. It underscores that strong leadership is essential to effectively implement new STEM standards and secure the long-term benefits for students. |

## Conclusions

Our initial discussion powerfully highlights a central challenge facing American education today: the pervasive, yet ambiguous use of the STEM acronym. Despite its popularity as a slogan, the term STEM frequently encompasses an extraordinary variety of meanings and initiatives, leading to confusion rather than clarity in its application. This chapter establishes the critical need for the educational community to transcend STEM as a mere label, urging the establishment of a clear, sustainable definition for its effective implementation in school programs and teaching practices. Fundamentally, this book aims to provide the necessary guidance to navigate these complexities, clarifying the rationale for STEM education and offering concrete directions for its programs and practices

## References

Fensham, P. J. (2009). Real world contexts in PISA science: Implication for context-based science education. *Journal of Research in Science Teaching*. Vol. 46(8): pp. 884–896.

Johnson, J., Richkind, J., & Ott, A. (2010). *Are we Beginning to See the Light?* New York: Public Agenda Survey.

Katehi, L., Pearson, G., & Feder, M. (Eds.) (2009). *Engineering in K-12 Education: Understanding the status and improving the prospects*. Washington, DC: National Academies Press.

Lichtenberg, J., Woock, C., & Wright, M. (2008). *Ready to Innovate: Are Educators and Executives Aligned on the Creative Readiness of the U.S. Workforce?* Conference Board, Research Report (2008). New York: Conference Board, Inc.

National Assessment Governing Board. (2013). *Technology and Engineering Literacy Framework for the 2014 National Assessment of Educational Progress*. Washington, DC: Author.

National Council of Teachers of Mathematics. (2000). *Principles and Standards for School Mathematics*. Reston, VA: Author.

National Governors Association Center for Best Practices & Council of Chief State School Officers. (2010). *Common Core State Standards for English Language Arts & Literacy in History/Social Studies, Science, and Technical Subjects and Common Core State Standards for Mathematics*. Washington, DC: Authors.

National Research Council (NRC). (2010). *Exploring the Intersection of Science Education and 21st Century Skills: A Workshop Summary*. Washington, DC: National Academies Press.

National Research Council. (2012). *A Framework for K-12 Science Education: Practices, Crosscutting Concepts, and Core Ideas*. Washington, DC: The National Academies Press.

NGSS Lead States. (2013). *Next Generation Science Standards: For States, By States*. Washington, DC: The National Academies Press.

# Part I
# STEM Education—Realities, Possibilities, and Priorities

# 2

# Realities

## STEM Is Here; and So Are Science Standards

This chapter introduces several realities associated with both STEM and new state standards for science. It aims to highlight important themes and challenges facing STEM education today. The chapter discusses how, despite its symbolic presence in American education, the acronym STEM has varying meanings and often lacks clear application in school programs and practices. It also explores the emergence of new state science standards like the Next Generation Science Standards (NGSS) and the complexities they introduce

---

Aim: To introduce important themes and challenge for contemporary STEM education.

Objectives: Individuals building changes for STEM education will:

- Learn about the challenges associated with reform based on STEM and new state standards, e.g., NGSS, and
- Identify opportunities based on programs that include opportunities from STEM and standards, respectively

Reflection:

- How would you define STEM for your school?
- What is your school or district already doing relative to STEM education?

for curriculum and instruction, including challenges in integrating all STEM disciplines and the realities limiting effective implementation.

The acronym STEM has attained a symbolic place in American education. In 2018, the US Postal Service released postage stamps for science, technology, engineering, and mathematics! The postage stamps notwithstanding, there still exist a need for clarification of STEM education in the specific contexts of school programs and classroom practices.

Coincidental with the emergence of STEM education a majority of states have adopted or adapted *Next Generation Science Standards* (*NGSS*) as a new state standard for science, most of which include engineering and recommend connections to mathematics. These standards reflect the influence of *Common Core States Standards* (CCCS, 2010), *A Framework for K-12 Science Education* (NRC, 2012) and the *NGSS* (NGSS Lead States, 2013).

There is a need for new instructional materials that address the realities of classroom teachers as they select, adapt, or develop instructional materials that align with new standards, many of which clearly include connections among the STEM disciplines.

## STEM Education: Several Realities

Although the acronym STEM is widely used, the meanings attributed to its use vary. For example, it may refer to a single discipline—science, the recognition of careers, a robotics competition, connections among the four disciplines, or a collective for the disciplines. We note that technology and engineering are downplayed even though they are part of many state standards. This reality results in an inconsistency as the acronym is applied to actual policies, programs, and practices for formal and informal education.

While STEM education has gained popularity among policy makers and many educators, it is not without critics. For example, in a 2010 piece for the *New York Times*, Natalie Angier argued that the acronym STEM was at best confusing, and may even be misleading. The weakness of STEM as a slogan and the failure of educators to clarify the acronym's meaning have been recognized in prior publications (e.g., Bybee, 2018). The ambiguous and diverse applications of the slogan do not help bring clarity to STEM. In fact, Marc Tucker (2012) suggested STEM makes no sense. Mr. Tucker's article draws comparisons to the high-performing countries in assessments such as Trends in International Mathematics and Science Study (TIMSS) and Programme for International Student Assessment (PISA). He places challenges on the science and math education of teachers, the school curriculum, and state assessments. The point that Tucker makes is that the educational system in other countries, not a specific STEM program, supports the higher achievement of students.

A 2010 survey by Entertainment Industries Council (Dyak et al., 2010) asked about 5000 individuals representing samples of individuals with high school diplomas, some college, college degrees, Master's, and PhDs whether or not they were familiar with the term "STEM education." Slightly more than 86% of participants indicated they were unfamiliar with the term. This result is reasonable, but not alarming given the fact that the survey results were reported in 2010, in the early phase of the use of the acronym. Recognition of STEM has very likely increased since this date.

Has the perception of STEM education changed? A 2018 report from the PEW Research Center (Funk & Parker, 2018) surveyed the American public's recognition of the acronym may have increased. However, it also reported that most Americans positively evaluated how well the K-12 public schools teach reading, writing, and mathematics, but assessed STEM education as "middling" (i.e., ordinary, mediocre or moderate in quality). Just more than 30% of adults believe STEM education in the US is below average, compared to other developed nations. In the same comparison, 42% rated US STEM education as average.

In results directly related to the themes and practical solutions presented in this book, the PEW survey reported the following as problems:

- Teachers do not emphasize the practical uses of STEM subjects in everyday life (53%).
- Teachers rarely use methods that help students think critically and solve problems (49%).
- Too little time spent on STEM subjects in elementary school (48%).
- Teachers do not have up-to-date curriculum materials (48%).

Rather than placing the blame on teachers, we support them in addressing a variety of challenges by emphasizing the applications of STEM disciplines, providing the means to help students think critically, increasing the time on STEM subjects in elementary grades, and facilitating the development and implementation of STEM units. These are opportunities for practical solutions that can be orchestrated by classroom teachers and the STEM education community.

Table 2.1 summarizes three challenges that likely will limit a long-term, sustained place for STEM in American education.

**TABLE 2.1** Challenges within STEM Education

| Ambiguity | ♦ Although widely used, the acronym has diverse meanings and lacks identifiable purposes. |
|---|---|
| Inconsistency | ♦ The application of STEM to policies, programs, and practices is inconsistent and varies across fundamental components of the education system |
| Incomplete representation of the disciplines | ♦ Often, not all STEM disciplines are not represented in school programs and instructional materials; this is especially true for technology and engineering. |
| Difficulty integrating the four disciplines | ♦ The integration of STEM presents a significant curricular and instructional issue. |

## Standard-based Science Education: Several More Realties

The architecture and expected outcomes of the *NGSS* differ significantly from the 1996 *National Science Education Standards* and also from state standards developed before 2013. In the *NGSS*, science and engineering practices, disciplinary core ideas, and crosscutting concepts form the three dimensions of learning. The objectives of the learning outcomes associated with the three dimensions are clearly identified by performance expectations—statements of competency that describe the content and skills to be assessed following instruction.

A comprehensive instructional program should provide opportunities for students to develop their understanding of disciplinary core ideas through their engagement in science and engineering practices and their application of crosscutting concepts. This three-dimensional learning leads to eventual mastery of performance expectations. A high-quality science program should clearly describe how the cumulative learning experience works coherently to build scientific literacy.

The following innovations in the *NGSS* are hallmarks of current thinking about how students learn science, and they set a vision for science education. These innovations will not only cause a shift in instructional programs and practices in American classrooms but also affect and refocus the efforts of curriculum developers and the design of comprehensive school science programs:

- ♦ Teaching to three dimension—science and engineering practices, crosscutting concepts, and disciplinary core ideas,

- Having students engage in explaining natural phenomena and solving design problems,
- Introducing science practices and crosscutting concepts in ways that include engineering and the nature of science,
- Including units or yearlong programs based on coherent learning progressions, and
- Making connections to mathematics and literacy standards.

The major innovations presented in contemporary state standards such as *NGSS* present a complex array of changes for curriculum and instruction, and especially for the decisions of classroom teachers. Some of the innovations are directly related to STEM disciplines, such as, for example, the practices of engineering design and using mathematics and computational thinking. Unfortunately, the complexity of standards results in the omission of some innovations as they are translated into instructional materials. Here, the role of crosscutting concepts in *NGSS* serves as a significant example.

In some cases, states have omitted specific standards or not adopted *NGSS* because they included politically, but not scientifically controversial topics such as biological evolution and climate change. The misperception that new standards were national mandates also resulted in the lack of adoption of *NGSS*.

Table 2.2 describes several realities influencing the implementation of *NGSS* and state standards based on *A Framework for K-12 Science Education* (NRC, 2012) and *NGSS*). The challenges center on the design of instructional materials and connect to the required knowledge and skills for teaching the innovative program.

**TABLE 2.2** Realities Limiting Implementation of *NGSS* and New State Standards

| Complexity | ◆ The five innovations present a complex array of changes for educators, especially those responsible for school programs, classroom instruction, and assessment. |
|---|---|
| Translation | ◆ The concerns of classroom teachers center on implications of standards for curriculum and instruction, assessment and accountability. |
| Controversy | ◆ Some states have not adopted *NGSS* for political reasons that center on selected content and perceptions concerning development and implementation of the standards. |
| Deficiency | ◆ The standards only give marginal recognition to significant personal and societal issues. |

- The five innovations present a complex array of changes for educators, especially those responsible for school programs, classroom instruction, and assessment.
- The concerns of classroom teachers center on implications of standards for curriculum and instruction, assessment and accountability.
- Some states have not adopted *NGSS* for political reasons that center on selected content and perceptions concerning development and implementation of the standards.
- The standards only give marginal recognition to significant personal and societal issues.

## Conclusion

To conclude, there are realities about STEM education that educators must face. While STEM education has potential it remains a slogan, and the dominant perceptions of the larger educational community are on standards-based science education.

> **Questions for Discussion:**
>
> - Are there other realities you would consider? If so, what are they?
> - Are the additional realities Purposes (i.e., goals)?, Policies (i.e., plans)?, Programs (i.e., instructional materials, assessments)?, or Practices (i.e., instructional models or strategies)?

## References

Angier, N., (2010). *STEM Education has Little to Do with Flowers*. New York OpEd, October 4, 2010.

Bybee, R. W. (2018). *STEM Education Now More Than Ever*. Arlington, VA: National Science Teachers Association (NSTA) Press.

Council of Chief State School officers (CCSSO). (2010). *Common Core State Standards* (CCSS). Washington, DC: National Governors Association.

Dyak, B., Keefe, B., & Brinton, L. J. (2010). *STEM: Analysis, Issues, and Future Directions*. Reston, VA: Entertainment and Media Communications Institute (A Division of Entertainment Industries Council, Inc.).

Funk, C., & Parker, K. (2018). *Most Americans Evaluate STEM Education as Middling Compared With Other Developed Nations*. Washington, DC: PEW Research Center.

National Research Council (NRC). (2012). *A Framework for K-12 Science Education: Practices, Crosscutting, Concepts, and Core Ideas*. Washington, DC: The National Academies Press.

NGSS Lead States. (2013). *Next Generation Science Standards: For States, By States*. Washington, DC: The National Academies Press.

Tucker, M. (2012). *STEM: Why It Makes No Sense*. Blog, June 19, 2012.

# 3

# Possibilities

## Thinking Differently About STEM Education

This chapter explores possibilities for STEM, NGSS, and new state standards. The discussion has implications for STEM education and the role of new school programs and teaching practices.

> Aim: To review opportunities to provide reasonable and achievable reforms that address contemporary STEM education and standards-based realities.
>
> Objectives: Individuals guiding possible changes for education in their state, district, or school will:
>
> ♦ Recognize connections between STEM possibilities and the content of state standards, and
> ♦ Realize the role of curriculum-based professional learning.
>
> Reflections:
>
> ♦ How do you think about the possibilities of STEM education in your school, district, and state?

The coincidence of STEM popularity and emergence of new state standards presents possibilities for both STEM education and standards-based science education. The opportunity resides in the need for STEM to develop greater clarity through applications in school programs and classroom practices. The new generation of state standards requires instructional materials that connect students' experiences with meaningful topics. This combined approach requires changes in teachers' knowledge and skills. A response that accommodates these coincidences, at least in part, is the development and implementation of curriculum-based professional learning.

## STEM Education: Several Possibilities

At about the same time as the criticisms and surveys cited in the prior chapter (2010–2012), STEM educators were discussing possibilities for STEM. Moon and Rundell Singer (2012) suggested that it is time to bring STEM into focus. That is, the STEM community needs to broaden its view of STEM to include an assemblage of practices and processes that transcend the specific STEM disciplinary boundaries. They extend this point to include the NGSS crosscutting concepts, for example. The authors make the following point,

> Moving STEM from a conundrum and a loose affiliation of disciplines to a powerful domain for structuring K-16 learning based upon a coherent set of practices and crosscutting concepts appears to be within our collective reach. This is the moment to build on the assembled wisdom now being conveyed.
> (Moon & Rundell Singer, 2012, p. 24)

In 2015, Ann Myers and Jill Berkowicz made the case that STEM broadens the school curriculum in ways that change the 20th-century mindset of individual disciplines toward the integration of disciplines central to advancement in the 21st century. Here is a pivotal quote from their article:

> What we call a STEM shift—a movement toward comprehensive and fully integrated STEM education throughout a school or district—is the first real and promising development with the potential to re-envision educational orientations from the bottom up. A STEM shift encourages the re-imagination of schools…including the way curriculum is designed, organized, and delivered. Done well, this includes the learning processes of inquiry, imagination, questioning, problem solving, creativity, invention, and collaboration – and certainly learning, thinking, and writing.
> (Myers & Berkowicz, 2015a, p. 18)

Several points are worth noting in this article and quote. The authors underscore the importance of integration, encourage a bottom-up approach, and emphasize the practices of the STEM disciplines.

To the aforementioned possibilities we would add the goal of students learning how to engage in civil discourse with their colleagues. Although not a K-12 discussion, Senchina (2010) provides a helpful model for weaving science and civics through interdisciplinary courses.

Another possibility is the STEM Schools Project (Meeder Consulting Group, 2012) which describes the processes and programs that schools use to create a STEM culture. In 2012, they recognized Project Lead the Way (PLTW) as a high-quality program that made positive inroads in schools and districts across the US. It is especially important to recognize the fact that PLTW represents a great opportunity to recognize the T and E in STEM education.

Although a 2012 article may not read like possibilities, indeed it is just that. We begin with the title "Teaching STEM Means Teacher Learning." The article tells the story of three teachers who began teaching STEM units they developed. Their initial efforts did not work very well. The three teachers appealed to an instructor at a local university for assistance because they had the courage to continue in spite of the initial difficulties. With the support of a professional developer and their own learning, the teachers realized the opportunity and so did their students. The lessons learned included: transitioning to new content and approaches requires teachers to go beyond their comfort zone; making the transition requires professional assistance and personal learning; shifting to STEM also required students to learn in new and different ways (O'Neill, Yamagata, Yamagata, & Togioka, 2012). The lessons learned supported several priorities of what we propose in later chapters.

This section concludes on other potentially positive possibilities. Jody Peterson, NSTA (National Science Teaching Association) assistant executive director for communications and legislative affairs, presents a new initiative, *Every Student Succeeds with STEM* (Peterson, 2017). Based on the Every Student Succeeds legislation, Ms. Peterson discussed plans and priorities for the STEM community. Included on the list of priorities are developing critical thinking and problem solving, workforce skills, and addressing equality issues.

The possibilities of STEM education certainly serve as a counterpoint to the potential limiting factors summarized in the prior chapter. Table 3.1 summarizes the key points of STEM possibilities.

## NGSS and State Standards: Several More Possibilities

For the possibilities discussion, since the late 1980s educators in the United States have recognized educational standards as expression of content and

**TABLE 3.1** Possibilities for STEM Education

| Opportunities | ♦ STEM initiatives can address omissions of national, state, and local standards. There are possibilities for innovative approaches such as place-based, problem-based, or project-based learning. |
|---|---|
| Support | ♦ The political support for STEM is strong, especially from policy makers, business, and industry. |
| Applications | ♦ Many challenges and potential solutions of the 21st century require understandings based on the STEM disciplines and contemporary content in state standards. |

processes for learning outcomes. Contemporary state standards build on this three-decade tradition of acceptance, and implementation of standards in curriculum, instruction, assessments, and learning.

State standards have significant influence on selection and teacher's professional implementation of instructional materials, licensure for teachers, design of state assessments, graduation requirements and, in most cases, the professional learning of teachers. Because states have the right to set standards and there is local control about the implementation of those standards, much of the controversy associated with the misperception of nationally imposed standards is avoided. In short, state standards avoid some, but not all, controversy.

The fact that a majority of states have either adopted *NGSS* or developed standards that are based on *A Framework for K-12 Science Education* (NRC, 2012). *NGSS* has the possibility of increasing coherence of the content and the skills expected of all students. To the degree the coherence increases the school programs and instructional practices, there is the possibility of increased scores on national and international assessments.

Although there are challenges to the implementation of contemporary standards, as we have seen for STEM education, there also are important opportunities. Table 3.2 summarizes several positive possibilities about state standards.

## Balancing Realities and Possibilities

As we have discussed, both STEM and Standards have realities and possibilities. Incorporating features of each can contribute to stronger school programs and teaching practices. The identifiable challenges to STEM education

# 4

# Priorities

## Reasonable and Prudent Recommendations for STEM Education

This chapter introduces important considerations for STEM education. We think the recommendations are grounded in common educational sense, appropriate for classroom teachers, and wise for practical matters of reforming STEM programs and instructional practices.

> Aim: To provide recommendations and initial answers to the question: What should be on a short list of priorities for implementing STEM education?
>
> Objectives: Individuals initiating changes involving STEM education should consider:
>
> - Fundamental knowledge of STEM disciplines,
> - Goals,
> - Design of instructional materials,
> - State standards, and
> - Curriculum-based professional learning.
>
> Reflection:
>
> - Suppose your principal asked you for the priorities in order to implement a STEM program. What would you list?

Chapter 3, on possibilities, concluded with a discussion of balancing the realities and possibilities of STEM education and state standards for education. We think the time is right for recognizing the need to a reform based on relatively recent state standards and the critical need to educate students about STEM-related personal, social, and global issues.

In this chapter we briefly present four priorities that are elaborated in subsequent chapters. The proposed priorities address: concerns about the current limits and future possibilities of STEM education; anxiety about the current political environment; a disregard by many for facts, evidence, and knowledge in general; and the historical and contemporary benefits of science, technology, engineering, and mathematics.

## First, Consider Fundamentals

A first step in pursuit of the vision involves increasing your understanding of the distinguishing features of the STEM disciplines (refer to Chapters 5 through 8).

We encourage you to review these chapters with the aim of clarifying and differentiating the STEM disciplines from each other and from other ways, i.e., explaining phenomena, adapting by humans, designing solutions, and quantifying relationships. For example, how are the respective STEM disciplines different from the arts? Philosophies? At a deeper level, how are the STEM disciplines different from each other?

## Second, Clarify Purposes

What are the broad purposes of authentic STEM education? This question centers on goals. The larger, national sense of advancing STEM education focuses on three aims:

- Achieving higher levels of STEM literacy for all citizens,
- Developing a deep technical workforce – one that meets 21st-century needs, and
- Attaining an advanced research and development workforce with diverse individuals in STEM careers.

To be more specific, STEM literacy includes the conceptual understandings and procedural skills and abilities needed for all individuals to address

STEM-related personal, social, and global issues. For example, STEM education would involve the basic concepts and processes of STEM disciplines and include appropriate content from standards. Education for STEM literacy would address the following goals:

- Acquire scientific, technological, engineering, and mathematical knowledge and use that knowledge to competently identify issues, acquire new knowledge, and apply the knowledge to STEM-related issues.
- Understand the characteristic features of STEM disciplines as forms of human endeavors that include the processes of inquiry, design, and analysis.
- Recognize how STEM disciplines contribute to our material, intellectual, and cultural world.
- Engage in STEM-related personal and social issues as concerned, effective, and constructive citizens.

(Adapted from Bybee, 2020)

Relative to the term authentic, in Mike Schmoker's 2019 recommendations, his recommendation to focus on authentic literacy had specific references to reading, writing, and discussion. While we certainly recognize the importance of these basics, we expand the use of authentic to include: (1) life situations such as public health, resources, environments, and hazards that are directly related to STEM, and (2) processes that require students to make sense of the life situations by emphasizing a model of claim–evidence–reason in their discussions, reports, and presentations (See, e.g., Brown et al. (2023)).

## Third, Review Options and Decide on Instructional Materials

The current marketplace offers limited examples of high-quality, well-aligned instructional materials for STEM education. Curriculum reform must therefore be accomplished through a systemic approach that requires educators to adapt current curricula select from limited or develop instructional options materials and learn new ways of using them. Putting curriculum reforms into practice is a difficult and demanding process that requires a vision of reform, support for change, collaboration among teachers to learn, and guidance at different levels (Anderson, 1995). Contemporary instructional materials of high-quality incorporate research on learning and challenge teachers to think differently about learning and teaching content knowledge and practices of the STEM disciplines. In addition to outlining what to teach, these materials must provide support for research-based instructional activities, incorporate standards, and include meaningful topics that engage students.

We acknowledge the challenges of addressing the list for high-quality instructional materials. That said, teachers demand materials they can use in their classrooms, and the supply is short. Clearly, "Instructional materials are the concrete resources that teachers use to plan, implement, and assess students' learning outcomes" (Short & Hirsh, 2022, p. 6).

Details on instructional materials will be elaborated in later chapters. Here, we present several recommendations for your consideration. Decisions about instructional materials should be guided by the following criteria.

- The scale of the materials should accommodate the needs of classroom teachers. For example, a single lesson or two would probably be too small and a full course would likely be too large. It seems to us that a unit expresses an achievable scale.
- The content should be basic. Look to the STEM fundamentals and the basic content of your state standards.
- The topic of materials should be meaningful for students. For example, local problems, interesting projects, and place-based contexts expresses our recommendation.
- The instructional strategies should be effective and based on research. For example, the 5E Instructional Model (Bybee, 2015) or the *Explore Before Explain* (Brown, 2019) might be used.

This discussion presents another priority: connecting teachers professional learning to the implementation of STEM-based curriculum materials. Teachers' knowledge and skills have as much of an effect on student learning as the choice of or development of instructional materials (Chingos & Whitehurst, 2012).

## Fourth, Establish Curriculum-Based Professional Learning

In *Science Teachers' Learning: Enhancing Opportunities, Creating Supportive Contexts* (NRC, 2015), Suzanne Wilson and her colleagues state that few K-12 science teachers have the expertise needed to teach the science required in the NGSS. On a positive note, they also declare that the "NGSS represents a fundamental change in the way science is taught and, if implemented well, will ensure that all students gain mastery over core concepts of science that are foundational to improving their scientific capacity" (p. 1). The authors

**TABLE 4.1** Priorities for STEM Education

| Consider Fundamentals | ♦ Begin with a review of fundamentals of science, technology, engineering, and mathematics.<br>♦ Establish achievable changes for curriculum, instruction, assessment, and professional development in your education system. |
|---|---|
| Clarify Purposes | Pursue three goals:<br>♦ STEM literacy for K-12 students as future adult citizens<br>♦ STEM skills and abilities for the 21st century workforce, and<br>♦ STEM research development and innovations as careers |
| Instructional Materials | ♦ Emphasize STEM as a complement to state standards.<br>♦ Select or design instructional materials with appropriate scale, connections to standards, engaging contexts, and effective instructional sequences. |
| Professional Learning | ♦ Few teachers are prepared with the knowledge and skills to select or design and develop instructional materials aligned with STEM.<br>♦ Implement curriculum-based professional learning |

conclude that teachers will need scientific knowledge and skills, instructional approaches, and instructional materials to implement *NGSS*-aligned strategies in their classrooms. "To enable teachers to acquire this kind of learnings," they write, "will in turn require profound changes to current systems for supporting teachers' learning across their careers, including induction and professional development" (p. 2).

Although this report centered on science standards, it could also apply to the expertise needed for STEM education. The challenge of incorporating state standards in STEM instructional materials is an invitation to establish "curriculum-based professional learning that focuses on the implementation of high-quality instructional materials…" (Short & Hirsh, 2022, p. 16).

Priorities and proposals are summarized in Table 4.1.

## Conclusion

Priorities center the vision on critical elements at the instructional core: first, there are content connections between STEM and new state standards; second, STEM-based instructional materials that would engage students in meaningful learning; and third, curriculum-based professional development designed to increase teachers' knowledge and skills. To be specific, we recommend involving teams of classroom teachers in the processes of designing, developing, and implementing STEM instructional materials. The materials would be developed across a series of professional learning experiences and involve facilitation by professional developers.

> **Questions for Discussion:**
>
> - What are the top priorities for your school? Students? Community?
> - What would be a reasonable and prudent initial effort?
> - Who should guide the effort?
> - What approvals will be important?

## References

Anderson, R. D. (1995). Curriculum reform: Dilemmas and promise. *Phi Delta Kappan*, Vol. 77(1): pp. 33–36.

Brown, P. L. (2019). Explore-before-explain. *Science & Children*, Vol. 56(9): pp. 38–42.

Brown, P. L., McTighe, J., & Bybee, R. W. (2023). Explore-before-explain. *Science & Children*, Vol. 56(9): pp. 38–42.

Bybee, R. W. (2015). *The BSCS Instructional Model: Creating Teachable Moments*. Arlington, VA: NSTA Press.

Bybee, R. W. (2020). *STEM, Standards, and Strategies for High Quality Units*. Arlington, VA: NSTA Press.

Chingos, M., & Whitehurst, G. (2012). *Choosing Blindly: Instructional Materials, Teacher Effectiveness and the Common Core*. Washington, DC: Brown Center on Education Policy, Brookings Institution. http://brookings.edu/research/reports/2012004/10-curriculum-chingos-whitehurst

National Research Council. (2015). *Science Teachers' Learning: Enhancing Opportunities, Creating Supportive Contexts*. Washington, DC: The National Academies Press.

Short, J., & Hirsh, S. (2022). *Transforming Teaching Through Curriculum-based Professional Learning: The Elements*. Thousand Oaks, CA: Corwin Press.

# Part II
# Introducing Foundations for the STEM Disciplines

# 5

# Science

## A Way of Explaining Phenomena in the World

The processes of science begin with questions about the natural or human designed world and proceeds by gathering evidence to be used as the basis for answering the questions.

> Aim: To provide an initial definition and useful description for science.
>
> Objectives: Individual teachers and others providing leadership for STEM education will:
>
> - Acquire introductory knowledge and understanding of science.
> - Develop an appreciation of the connections of science with other STEM disciplines.
>
> Reflection:
>
> - How would you explain how science works to a colleague?
> - What is the role of evidence in science?

This chapter introduces basic ideas about science. The formal category of these ideas: "the nature of science." An informal characterization is "How science works." Specifically, the emphasis is on "rules" for differentiating science from other ways of knowing.

Recommendations that science teachers introduce ideas about science as a complement to the body of accumulated scientific knowledge are not new; yet this approach seems especially important now. The presentation in this chapter extends, and is based on, a long history of prior publications (see, for example, Lederman, 1986; McComas, 2004; Clough, 2000; Lederman, 2007; Duschl, 1985, 1988, 1990; Bybee et al., 1992a, 1992b; Wahbeh & Abd-El-Khalick, 2014; Showalter, 1974; Klopfer & Cooley, 1963; Allchin, 2012; Osbourn et al., 2003).

This chapter anticipates discussions of technology, engineering, and mathematics and a detailed discussion of the nature of science in the *Next Generation Science Standards* (NGSS/Lead States, 2013).

The word "science" is derived from the Latin "scientia," meaning knowledge. Definitions of science generally include such description as: an organized body of knowledge, a systematic, objective search for understanding of the natural world, a body of knowledge derived from methods based on an empirical approach, statements of generality and tests to evaluate the veracity of knowledge. In this section, I develop a simple, yet comprehensive description—science as a way of explaining phenomena in the natural world. I paraphrased the phrase from John Moore's phrase—science as a way of knowing (Moore, 1993).

Science for All Americans (AAAS, 1989) describes the nature of science along the following lines:

> Over the course of human history, people have developed many interconnected and validated ideas about the physical, biological, psychological, and social worlds. Those ideas have enabled successive generations to achieve an increasingly comprehensive and reliable understanding of the human species and its environment. The means used to develop these ideas are particular ways of observing, thinking, experimenting, and validating. These ways represent a fundamental aspect of the nature of science and reflect how science tends to differ from other modes of knowing.
>
> (p. 25)

This quotation summarizes the nature of science and points out the theme of science as a way of phenomena in explaining the natural world. I prefer science as a way of explaining the natural world. The phrase "science as a way of explaining phenomena in the natural world" concisely presents what students should understand about the nature of science. It suggests that science is *a* way of explaining, rather than *the* way of explaining. I am using the word "way" as a course of action, habits of mind, sets of processes, practices, or procedures. The phrase "way of explaining" conveys the idea that science is an ongoing process that focuses on developing and organizing knowledge. A simple, yet dynamic quality to the phrase conveys much more than the definition of science as both products (i.e., new knowledge) and processes (i.e., inquiry).

Scientific knowledge changes continuously. Two types of changes occur in the development of scientific explanations. First, new explanations for phenomena are proposed. Second, current explanations are modified based on new evidence. In recent decades, the changes in scientific explanations have occurred as increasing rates and in varied directions. Scientific knowledge is revised, expanded, and elaborated based on different observations, better technologies, or new experimental results—evidence. Theories may be replaced or advanced as a result of crucial observations, experiments, evidence, and new theoretical insights.

Change in scientific knowledge is governed by the values of science and the methods and processes scientists use. The nature of science is a dynamic relationship between three factors: The extant body of scientific knowledge—products; the values of science—standards for acceptance of new knowledge; and the processes of scientific inquiry—methods of investigation that produce evidence.

The scientific enterprise works to produce a body of knowledge consisting of descriptions and interpretations of the natural world on which the scientific community agrees. A basic tenet of the scientific community, and one that assumes the development of new explanations, is the tentative nature of scientific knowledge.

The procedures and standards reflect the values shared by the community of scientists. Those values include honesty, precision, verifiability, and parsimony.

The methods of science are difficult to describe outside the context of specific investigations. There is not one single scientific method, nor is there a fixed set of steps that scientists always follow. Methods differ among the science disciplines depending upon the type and stage of scientific investigation and whether the question requires evidence from a descriptive, an experimental, or a theoretical approach. The methods of science common to scientists include observation, measurement, hypothesis formulation and testing, data collection, experimental investigation, and prediction. Once acquired, data must be organized, summarized, and interpreted in meaningful ways. Some examples of meaningful data summaries include taxonomies of organisms, the periodic table, and classifications of rocks and minerals. The next section gives a more detailed description of the nature of scientific knowledge.

## Nature of Scientific Explanations

Scientists share a set of assumptions about the world. They believe, for example, that phenomena in the natural world are explainable. The universe is not capricious, and patterns in nature generally reflect an underlying order in the universe. Scientists also assume that they can discover more about the world through systematic study and the application of instruments and the intellect.

Scientists also assume that the universe is a single system containing numerous subsystems. The natural laws for one time and location on the Earth apply at other times and locations. For example, the law of gravitation applied in the past also applies now. Another assumption is that knowledge gained from studying one portion of the universe is applicable to other parts of the universe. Again, the laws of gravity are the same for the Earth as they are for other planets (AAAS, 1989). The following sections briefly escribe several factors from a list of many that illustrate the nature of scientific knowledge.

### Scientific Explanations are Both Tentative and Stable
The processes of science produce evidence which scientists use as the basis for explanations. Scientific explanation may change based on new experiments that result in evidence and, subsequently, explanations that challenge current explanations. Explanations in science are neither absolute nor complete; if anything, they are probable and tentative. Science does not prove anything once and for all time. Scientific explanation enables one to make probabilistic statements about objects and events in the world.

Although scientific explanations are tentative, they can prove durable. The processes of science often result in the modification and reconstruction of ideas rather than outright rejection. Powerful explanations tend to remain and develop while less powerful explanations are revised or discarded.

### Scientific Explanations are Made Public
One assumption scientists hold is that other scientists can eventually arrive at the same explanations if they have access to similar experiences and evidence. Therefore, scientists make their findings and their methods public via presentations at meetings and professional publications, for example.

### Scientific Explanations Can Inform and Provide Predictions
Scientific explanations not only help answer immediate questions, but should also have the ability to predict, to show relationships not explained previously. A powerful explanation not only fits the specific observations of a

particular experiment; it should also fit other observations. The predictions could relate to the past, such as fossil evidence, or the future, such as the chances of pandemics or the prospects for climate change.

### Scientific Explanations are Based on Evidence

Observation and experimentation provide evidence that is the basis of scientific explanations. The validations of refutation of scientific knowledge is based on evidence from the natural world. Knowledge claims are tested through empirical validation. Scientists attempt to get, and report, accurate data. They obtain data through measurements in natural settings, such as an ecosystem, and in laboratories. In many instances, they use instruments (technologies) to help them extend their senses and obtain precise observations. Science teachers introduce the role of controlled experiments as a key to producing evidence supporting a proposed explanation. Although important, controlled experiments are not always possible due to practical, ethical, or procedural circumstances. Still, scientists rely on evidence and testable models for their proposed explanations.

### Scientific Evidence is Replicable

Scientists working in different places at different times should be able to repeat another scientist's observations and experiments and derive the same evidence.

### Scientific Explanations are Strengthened by Accumulated Evidence

Scientific knowledge is cumulative and developmental. Knowledge from the past is the basis for presenting scientific explanations, which is the subsequent basis for future explanations. Like the development of organisms, there may be characteristics at one period and significant change from that period to the next. Historical explanations must be examined in the context of the historic period, rather than being evaluated in the light of contemporary understanding. Similarly, contemporary scientific explanations should be understood in technological, mathematical, and social contexts.

### Scientific Explanations are Limited

There are at least two ways in which scientific explanations may be limited. First, technology often limits the quality and quantity of data for proposed explanations. Second, some questions are simply beyond the parameters of science. In many instances, science provides explanations for what we *can* do, and not for what we *ought* to do. The latter falls into the other domains, such as those of philosophy, theology, and politics.

## Conclusion

Science teachers have been concerned primarily with teaching the facts, information, concepts, principles, and theories of science, and, to a much lesser degree, theories of technology. This chapter is about science. The next chapters are about technology/engineering. As STEM educators, we have to answer the questions—What is it about science that is important for students to know and value? Another way to think about this discussion is that it answers questions teachers are frequently asked by students—What is science? And what is technology? The presentations in this chapter and the next illuminate the relationship between science and technology—a relationship that is becoming increasingly important in society and yet is not at all clear in extant science programs.

One purpose of STEM education is to help all students develop an understanding of STEM disciplines. Most students today, however, do not understand science and usually cannot distinguish science from technology; in fact, they often confuse the two. The following definitions provide a distinction between science and technology, offering a way for students to begin developing deeper and clearer understandings.

- Science proposes *explanations for observations* about the natural world.
- Technology proposes *solutions for problems* of human adaptation to the environment.

Science originates in questions about the world. How do earthquakes occur? What is causing global warming? How do plants make food? Scientists are a recognized, through variable processes of rational inquiry. The word "explanations" is synonymous with knowledge claims and the goals of understanding scientific concepts and theories. Explanations proposed by scientists relate to observations about the natural world and imply that humans have questions about objects, organisms, and phenomena they observe: "Why is the sky blue?," "Why do I look like my brother?," Why do objects fall?" These are typical questions young students ask about the world. "What are the causes and consequences of global climate change?," "How did the global pandemic occur?," "What is the basic structure of the human genome?," "What occurs in a black hole?" These are questions scientists ask. They phrase questions in a more sophisticated language and propose more complex answers, but their investigations begin with a question to which they subsequently propose an evidence-based answer. In his 1989 book, *The Privilege of Being a Physicist*, Victor Weisskopf highlights the central role of scientific questions:

Science is curiosity, discovering things and asking why. Why is it so? Indeed, science is the opposite of knowledge. Science asks the why and how questions and therefore is the process of questioning not the acquisition of information. We must always begin by asking questions, not by giving answers. We must create interest in things, phenomena, and processes.

(p. 31)

In short, scientific questions and answers center on explanations for the whys and hows of objects, organisms, and events in the world.

---

**Questions for Discussion:**

- How can you incorporate the nature of science into a STEM program?
- How would you explain a rationale for the nature of science to a school administrator?

---

## References

Allchin, D. (2012). Toward clarity on whole science and knows. *Science Education*, Vol. 96(4): pp 693–700.

American Association for the Advancement of Science (AAAS). (1989). *Science for All Americans*. New York: Oxford University Press.

Bybee, R. W., Geise, J., Ellis, J., & Parse, L. (1992a). *Teaching About the History and Nature of Science and Technology: A Curriculum Framework*. Colorado Springs, CO: BSCS.

Bybee, R. W., Geise, J., Ellis, J., & Parse, L. (1992b). *Teaching About the History and Nature of Science and Technology: Background Papers*. Colorado Springs, CO: BSCS.

Clough, M. (2000). The nature of science: Understanding how the game of science is played. *The Clearing House*, Vol. 74(1): pp. 13–17.

Duschl, R. (1985). Science education and the philosophy of science: Twenty-five years of mutually exclusive development. *School Science and Mathematics*, Vol. 85: pp. 541–555.

Duschl, R., (1988). Abandoning the scientific legacy of science education. *Science Education*, Vol. 72(1): pp. 55–62.

Duschl, R. (1990). *Restructuring Science Education: The Importance of Theories and Their Development.* New York: Teachers Colleges Press.

Klopfer, L., & Cooley, W. (1963). Effectiveness of the history of science cases for high school in the development of student understanding of science and scientists. *Journal of Research in Science Teaching*, Vol. 1: pp 35–47.

Lead States/NRC. (2013). *Next Generation Science Standards.* Washington, DC: The National Academies Press.

Lederman, N. (1986). Student's and teachers' understanding of the nature of science: A reassessment. *School Science and Mathematics*, Vol. 82(2): pp. 91–99.

Lederman, N. (2007). Nature of science: Past, present, and future. In Abell, S. & Lederman, N. (Eds.). *Handbook of Research on Science Education*, pp. 831–879. Mahwah, NJ: Lawrence Erlbaum Associates.

McComas, W. (2004). Keys to teaching the nature of science. *The Science Teacher*, Vol. 71(9): pp 24–27.

Moore, J. (1993). *Science as a Way of Knowing.* Cambridge, MA: Harvard University Press.

Osbourn, J., Collins, S., Ratcliff, M., Millar, R., & Duschl, R. (2003). What "ideas-about-science" should be taught in school science? A Delphi study of the expert community. *Journal of Research in Science Teaching*, Vol. 40(7): pp 692–720.

Showalter, V. (1974). Program objectives and scientific literacy. *Prism II*, Vol. 2(3 & 4), 1–4.

Wahbeh, N., & Abd-El-Khalick, F. (2014). Revisiting the translation of nature of science understandings into instruction practice: Teachers' nature of science pedagogical content knowledge. *International Journal of Science Education*, Vol. 36: pp 425–466.

# 6

# Technology

## A Way of Adapting by Humans

Technological innovations originate with human wants or needs and may result in information, communication, transportation, and associated artifacts. Technological innovations must accommodate human and natural constraints.

---

Aim: To provide an initial definition and useful description for technology.

Objectives: Individual teachers and others providing leadership for STEM education will:

- Gain introductory knowledge and understanding of technology.
- Realize connections of technology with other STEM disciplines.

Reflection:

- Beyond computers, what counts as technology?
- Why is technology important to individuals and society?

---

Take a moment and look around. Very likely you will see objects as simple as a paperclip or as complex as a car, computer, or solar cell. In recent years, citizens have used face masks and been vaccinated. Such medical technologies have protected people from infections and live healthier lives. Technological products and processes provide people with better transportation, communication, and health, among other things. Understanding the forms and functions of technology in personal and social perspectives in a general goal for this chapter.

The Greek word "techne," meaning art or craft, is the root of technology. Technology is commonly defined as the application of knowledge to solve practical problems. A broader, and perhaps more accurate, view of technology is the cultural knowledge or means to control the environment, extract resources, product objects, goods, and services, intended to sustain human existence and improve the quality of life; in short, to help humans adapt.

A quotation for *Science for All Americans* (AAAS, 1989) initiates development of the theme of technology as a way of adapting. The quotation is from the chapter on the nature of technology.

> As long as there have been people, there has been technology. Indeed, the techniques of shaping tools are taken as the chief evidence of the beginning of human culture. On the whole, technology has been a powerful force for the development of civilization, all the more so as its link with science has been forged. Technology—like language, ritual, values, commerce, and the arts—is an intrinsic part of a cultural system and it both shapes and reflects the system's values. In today's technology is a complex social enterprise that includes not only research, design, and crafts, but also finance, manufacturing, management, labor, marketing, and maintenance.
>
> In the broadest sense, technology extends our abilities to change the world: to cut, shape, or pull together materials; to move things from one place to another; to reach farther with our hands, voices, and senses. We use technology to try to change the world to suit us better. The changes may relate to survival needs, such as food, shelter, or defense, or they may relate to human aspirations, such as knowledge, art, or control. But the results of changing the world are often complicated and unpredictable. They can include unexpected benefits, unexpected costs, and unexpected risks—any of which my fall on different social groups at different times. Anticipating the effects of technology is therefore so important as advancing its capabilities.
>
> (AAAS, 1990, p. 25)

Technologies help solve human problems and achieve human aspirations. In the quotation from *Science for All Americans* (1990), there is the specific sentence, "We use technology to try to change the world to suit us better." This position parallels our point that technology originates in humans' need to adapt. Technology is not just to "suit us better." Our point is that technology represents a cultural variation on biological adaptations. Using adaptation as part of the definition of technology provides the dimension of intention to humans' development of technology.

Technology originates when humans identify problems by adapting. Stating this view another way, humans use the results of technological innovation to change their environment or overcome environmental barriers. We adapt by changing the environment and using technologies. The changes relate to human needs, including survival (for example, food, defense), communication, transportation, and higher needs such as the aesthetic aspirations of art. Humans need to communicate, grow food, and defend themselves. At the simplest levels, one can think of historical innovations, such as telegraph machines, plows, and guns. Or there are more complex technologies of facsimile machines, tractors, and the Strategic Defense Initiative. All of these examples point up the connections of technology and human adaptation.

Developing technological solutions requires consideration of materials, scientific laws, and the ability of humans to use the innovation. Certainly, inventors also consider other such as cost, performance criteria, efficiency, and aesthetics.

There are human aspects of technological problem solving that also apply to scientific inquiry. Those characteristics include curiosity, creativity, aesthetics, critical thinking, and reasoning. We also should point out several differences between science and technology: Scientists develop explanations about the world and technologists develop means to control the world; scientists develop explanations that are generalizable, and technologists develop solutions to specific problems; scientists attempt to show that explanations incorporate all observations, and technologists attempt to show that solutions work.

Students should understand that technology affects society directly because of the connection between technology, human problems, and the tangible products. Subsequently, citizens should consider the potential benefit or harm of technologies. Personal and social values and ethical judgments are inextricably related to technological innovation. Anna J. Harrison, in her 1984 presidential address to AAAS, was particularly clear on the benefits and burdens of technology:

> Society is not home free with the benefits of goods and services and the benefits of economic development. Every technological change, be it by transfer or by innovation and regardless of how great the positive impact on society, also has a negative impact. This is a statement of no proof. I have for some rears challenged audiences to cite examples of

technological change for which it is not true. The most apt reply so far was proposed by a West Point cadet who suggested the flyswatter.

(p. 940)

Technology, as mentioned above, is as old as humans. With the possible exception of some examples from nonhuman primates, the development and use of tools is one unique characteristic of humans. The primary goal of those who develop technologies is adaptation. Other expressions of this goal include extended the senses, thereby improving the quality of life, and bettering the human condition.

The phrase "technology as a way of adapting" has similar qualities and characteristics to the phrase "science as a way of explaining," simultaneously conveying a sense of both process and product. The phrase "way of adapting" broadens the meaning of technology, which is more than computers and CAT scanners. Through analysis, one can evaluate why a particular technology was designed and measure the effectiveness of various devices in achieving those purposes.

Technological innovation originates with a problem. The devices and processes used to resolve the problem are constrained by information, physical laws, and properties of materials. A number of other factors are involved, including societal values, aesthetics, costs, risks, and benefits. One of the essential underlying values of the process of developing technologies is efficiency: Getting the best device that has the greatest benefit, the lowest cost, and the least amount of risk.

## Technologies are Developed Within Natural Constraints

No technological innovation can contravene natural laws. Conservation of matter and energy, the laws of thermodynamics, and the physical properties of materials, such as flexibility and conductivity, are all examples of natural constraints on technological development.

### Technologies Involve Control

The goal of human adaptation with its attendant technological systems involves control. Comparison of what is happening with what ought to be happening within a system, and making appropriate adjustments, is the essence of technological control. Thermostats, automobiles, and airplanes are all examples of systems where there is input to the system, adjustment, output that results in further input, and so on. Control of heat, combustion rate, and speed, respectively, are controlled in the examples just cited.

## Technologies May Have Unintended Side Effects

Technologies are neither entirely beneficial nor detrimental. With each technological innovation, there are unintended consequences. Work can be made more efficient by a technology, but workers may suffer from its effects. It is difficult to predict all the outcomes of a new technology, which is the reason why engineers include risk–benefits analysis, and the government requires impact statements, the evaluation of new drugs, and the assessment of safety for new products.

Even with risk analysis, there are still effects that cannot be predicted because of the complexity of infrequent use of the technology. Individual reactions to risk and almost unrelated to probability modes that predict the risks. The degree to which any society depends on technology is also an expression of the degree to which that society must bear the burden of risk.

## Technologies Eventually Fail

With time, things break. Just as scientific explanations are not enduring, so technological solutions are not permanent. Materials wear, systems malfunction, and parts break, resulting in the eventual failure of technological systems. This idea extends to the complexity and use of technologies. The more complex a technological system, the greater the probability of failure and the more widespread the consequences of that failure.

# Relationships Among Science, Technology, and Engineering

The relationship between science and technology is more complex than suggested in this discussion. However, we think that an introduction to the nature of science and technology is most effective when the disciplines are presented in a clear and simple form. In the aforementioned presidential address by Anna J. Harrison, (1984), she mentioned the relationships among science, engineering, and technology. This section concludes with an extended quotation from Dr. Harrison's address:

> It is true that science drives engineering and technological innovation, but it is equally true that both engineering and technology drive science. The three processes, science, engineering, and technological innovation, are synergistic. Each is dependent on the other two: each supports the other two. It is this synergism that enhances the total capabilities of science, engineering, and technology. The productivity of this synergism is abundantly evident in the events that have and are propelling us into an information society. In rapidly developing

areas of new technology at the forefront of scientific knowledge, the distinction between science and engineering diminishes as scientists investigate how to solve problems as well as investigate phenomena as well as how to solve problems. Technology, of course, involves not only scientists and engineers but many others working together within an institutional structure essential to the production of goods and services.

(p. 940)

## Conclusion

Traditional definitions of technology, such as "applied science," are incomplete. Technology, which is more than an applied science and more than a method, originates in human problems of adaptation to the environment and results in proposed solutions to those problems. Problems, such as "How can we communicate better?," "How can we travel easier?," and "How can we protect ourselves?" are examples of technological problems.

Humans need protection and food, and they need to move objects and information from one place to another. The means used to fulfil these needs constitutes technology in its simplest form. Historical examples of technology, such as use of tools, development of agriculture, and use of weapons illustrate the definition of technology based on problems in human adaptation. I am using the noun "adaptation" in its general sense of the process of changing for a special use. In the biological sense, there is a genetic alteration. In the technological sense, humans alter or adjust the environment through objects and inventions. There are many possible solutions to problems in human adaptation, and inevitably there also are many variables and requirements that must be considered. Some of these are constraints, such as availability of materials, properties of materials, laws of thermodynamics, and societal requirements. Other variables include cost and performance criteria.

> **Question for Discussion:**
> ♦ What did you find most insightful about this chapter?

## References

AAAS. (1990). *Science for All Americans*. New York: Oxford University Press
American Association for the Advancement of Science. (1989). *Science for All Americans*. Washington, DC: Author.
Harrison, A. (1984). Common elements and interconnections. *Science*, Vol. 215: pp. 939–942.

# 7

# Engineering

## A Way of Designing Solutions for Human Problems

This chapter is closely related to the prior chapter on technology. Engineering can be summarized as "design under constraint."

> Aim: To provide an initial description and useful definition for engineering.
>
> Objectives: Individual teachers and others facilitating the implementation of STEM education will:
>
> - Acquire introductory knowledge and understanding of engineering.
> - Realize the connections among engineering and other STEM disciplines, especially technology.
>
> Reflection:
>
> - How would you define engineering for a colleague?
> - How does the chapter's title help with your initial thoughts?

Many individuals confuse the disciplines of science, technology, and engineering; and, by extension, the work of scientists, technologists, and engineers. Prior chapters have introduced fundamental knowledge about science and technology. This chapter continues with basic information about engineering.

We used several reports from the National Academy of Engineering as the basis for this discussion. Those reports included: *Engineering in K-12 Education* (NAE, 2009); *STEM Integration in K-12 Education* (NAE, 2014); *and Building Capacity for Teaching Engineering in K-12 Education* (NAE, 2020).

The word engineer is derived from the Latin word *ingeniare*, which means design. Engineer is also associated with the Latin word for engine, *ingenium*, which means a clever invention (NAE, 2009). So, an initial, brief definition of engineering is the process of designing unique inventions.

Engineering includes a body of knowledge and processes for solving problems. It is closely related to technology and can be summarized as "design under constraint." The constraints include natural laws, time, money, and quality of proposed solutions.

Although subtle, one should note that scientists endeavor to explain the natural world and that engineers attempt to solve problems to accommodate humans' needs and wants. In actuality, it is difficult to separate science, technology and engineering. Scientific knowledge informs engineering problem solving and technological tools and process. In turn, engineering design and subsequent technological products contribute to scientific advances.

## Engineering: Design as a Way of Solving Problems

This overview continues with an essential question—How is engineering defined? The National Academy of Engineering Report *Building Capacity for Teaching Engineering in K-12 Education* (NAE, 2020) answered the question as follows:

> Engineering is both a knowledge of the creation and design of human-made products and processes and a problem-solving method called design under constraint.
>
> (NAE, 2020, p. 31)

This definition includes knowledge and methods of engineering. That is, knowledge about products and processes of engineering. The definition highlights the problem solving method of design under constraint. The latter, engineering design, was discussed in *Standards for Technological Literacy: Content for the Study of Technology* (ITEA, 2000).

William Wulf, the past president of the National Academy of Engineering, also provides a useful and succent way to describe engineering—"design under constraint" (Wulf, 1998). As engineers design solutions, they operate within constraints, some of which must be considered—physical laws, such as conservation of energy, properties of materials, and knowledge of biological systems. Other constraints are more flexible, for example budget, regulations, production schedules and quality of solutions.

## Key Attributes for Engineering Design

The design process is guided by a number of core ideas, basic skills, and habits of mind.

> *Engineering design requires specifications.* What will the design process accomplish? What counts as a solution to the identified problem?
> *Engineering design must accommodate constraints.* The idea of constraints has been introduced, but it is worth restating. What are the limitations that absolutely must be considered (i.e., physical laws)? And what are those that have some potential for flexibility (i.e., economic, political, social, and ethical)?
> *Engineering design attempts to optimize and balance the criteria for a solution and confecting constraints.* How do engineers finally select the best solution from several alternatives? This process is called optimization.
> *Engineering design considers the trade-offs inherent in decisions about potential solutions to the problem.* An important aspect of engineering design includes a cost, risk, and benefit analysis.
> *Engineering design involves a number of characteristic stages.* It is generally understood that there is not a set number of steps for engineering design. There are, however, characteristic stages in the development of engineered solutions. An initial stage is identifying and clarifying the problem. What exactly is the goal? Next is a stage of generating possible solutions, perhaps using individual brainstorming and/or a team effort. This stage may result in a range of potential design solutions. This prior stage is followed by one of the evaluation of the proposed solutions to different models (i.e., physical, graphical, mathematical). Finally, data from the evaluation stage can be used to make a decision about how to proceed with a proposed solution. If necessary, these steps are repeated.

## Engineering and Technology and the Challenges of Contemporary Society

Since the emergence of engineering as a formal discipline in the middle of the 16th century, when the specialists replaced the work of artisans in the design of military fortifications, engineering has continued to expand as a discipline and in its influences on society. After the American Civil War engineering programs increasingly emphasized formal, academic education. Such formal education of engineers was in contrast to the more practical approach which centered on artisans and craftsmen who, through apprenticeships and on-the-job education, learned about the design and development of machines, and, in Britain, the infrastructure for a transportation system (NAE, 2009). This brief history introduces the origins of engineering as a formal discipline and the origin of technology as related and often complementary work In the United States, the 19th century witnessed the development of both the academic and practical pathways to both engineering and technology.

Across history, the roles of technology and engineering extended to varied domains. The primary processes which contributed to the discipline's expansion was problem solving as it relates to people's daily lives and the wider needs of society. So, we now have systems of transportation and communications, as well as self-driving cars. We also have systems for healthcare with devices to measure blood pressure, analyze blood samples, and magnetic resonance imaging (MRI) equipment to provide images for diagnosis of internal problems.

We have proposed two challenges for contemporary STEM education, both of which are based on scientific explanations and require both engineering design and technological solutions. The grand challenge we proposed was to provide knowledge and understanding of the global pandemic and climate change for K-12 students. As it turns out, the National Academy of Engineering (NAE) identified a list of 14 grand challenges for the 21st century. They noted that the solutions to these challenges are all significant engineering and technological input (see Table 7.1).

A brief review of the grand challenges for engineering (and technology) highlights the theme of problem solving and at least seven that are related to climate change (5) and the pandemic (2).

**TABLE 7.1** Grand Challenges for Engineering

In 2008, the National Academy of Engineering announced 14 "grand challenges for engineering," examples of the types of challenges confronting societies in the 21st century.
The 14 grand challenges are:

- Making solar power economical.
- Providing energy from fusion.
- Developing carbon-sequestration methods.
- Managing the nitrogen cycle.
- Providing access to clean water.
- Restoring and improving urban infrastructure.
- Advancing health informatics.
- Engineering better medicines.
- Reverse-engineering the brain.
- Preventing nuclear terror.
- Securing cyberspace.
- Enhancing virtual reality.
- Advancing personalized learning.
- Engineering the tools of scientific discovery.

## Conclusion

Although STEM education is not the full solution to the challenges, it must make a contribution. Thus, engineering and technology will not solve the challenges associated with the pandemic and climate change, but the challenges do require the use of engineering design as a process for solving contemporary challenges.

**Question for Discussion:**

- How is the design process different from scientific inquiry?

## References

NAE. (2020). *Building Capacity for Teaching Engineering in K-12 Education.* Washington, DC: The National Academies Press.

NAE and NRC. (2009). *Engineering in K-12 Education: Understanding the Status and Improving the Prospects.* Washington, DC: The National Academies Press.

NAE and NRC. (2014). *STEM Integration in K-12 Education: Status, Prospects, and Agenda for Research.* Washington, DC: The National Academies Press.

Wulf, W. A. (1998). The Urgency of Engineering Education. In *The Bridge.* Washington, D.C: National Academy of Engineering.

# 8

# Mathematics

## A Way of Quantifying and Expressing Relationships

Mathematics includes the study of patterns and relationships among quantities, numbers, and space. The possible relationships can be among abstractions without real-world connection. Mathematics may also express relationships between actual phenomena and potential applications in the natural or designated world.

> Aim: To provide an initial description and useful definition of mathematics.
>
> Objectives: Individual teachers and others facilitating reforms of STEM education will:
>
> - Learn introductory knowledge about the discipline of mathematics.
> - Realize connections of mathematics with other disciplines, i.e., science, technology and engineering.
>
> Reflection:
>
> - What is the role of mathematics in STEM education?
> - How is STEM-based mathematics different from traditional mathematics classes?

We live in a world saturated with numbers. News reports indicate the daily percent change in the stock market, the risk of diseases. The requirements of quantitative thinking extend beyond daily news to nearly every field of work, and especially to scientific, technological, and engineering disciplines. For many mathematicians, the essence of the discipline is in its elegance and intellectual challenge. For most citizens, however, the need to understand numbers lies not in mathematical beauty and logic, but in their practical value, expressed as quantitative literacy (Steen, 2001). In clear and extreme terms, Lynn Steen stated "an innumerate citizen today is as vulnerable as the illiterate peasant of Gutenberg's time" (Steen, 1997). Although published in 1997, this situation has only deepened in an age of social media.

> *Science for All Americans* (AAAS, 1990) provides insightful connection among mathematics and other disciplines, especially science; and, I would add, technology and engineering. The following discussion relies on ideas from *Science for All Americans* and their application to STEM.
> *Mathematics and science, an attempt to discover patterns and relationships*. Science, technology, and engineering provide mathematics with problems to solve, and mathematics provides science, technology, and engineering with means to analyze data. Both of these processes may occur in the investigation of patterns and relationships.
> *Mathematics provides a language for STEM*. The application of mathematical symbols such as $D = \frac{M}{V}$ is, for example, a clear statement of the quantitative relationship between the variable of matter and volume.
> *Mathematics and science, technology, and engineering share several assumptions*. The disciplines share the idea that phenomena are understandable due to an assumption of order. Other shared features include use of logic in explanations, honesty and public presentation of findings, and skeptical review by peers.
> *Mathematics, technology, and engineering have developed productive relationships*. While mathematics contributes to ways expressed by the phrase "mathematics is the language of science," it is also the case that mathematics contributes to engineering problem solving and technology by describing models of complex systems and the analysis of different proposed designs.

The urgent need for school programs to address grand challenges of public health and global climate suggests quantitative literacy as an especially important mathematical realm. To begin a discussion; quantitative literacy is neither abstract mathematics nor practical statistics. The book *Mathematics and Democracy: The Case for Quantitative Literacy* (NCED, 2001) presents the following clarification of quantitative literacy (i.e., numeracy).

> Quantitative literacy is more a habit of mind, an approach to problems that employs and enhances both statistics and mathematics. Unlike statistics, which is primarily about uncertainty, numeracy is often about the logic of certainty. Unlike mathematics, which is primarily about a platonic realm of abstract structures, numeracy is often anchored in data derived from and attached to the empirical world.
> (NCED, 2001, p. 5)

As individuals confront and try to understand the complexities of the grand challenges the role of numeracy certainly has a priority.

> Quantitatively literate citizens need to know more than formulas and equations. They need a predisposition to look at the world through mathematical eyes, to see the benefits (and risks) of thinking quantitatively about commonplace issues, and to approach complex problems with confidence in the value of careful reasoning. Quantitative literacy empowers people by giving them tools to think for themselves, to ask intelligent questions of experts, and to confront authority confidently. These are skills required to thrive in the modern world.
> (NCED, 2001, p. 3)

Citizens need to approach the complex problem of emerging and reemerging diseases and the personal and social consequences of climate change with confidence in the value of clear and careful reasoning. Unfortunately, this often is not the case. While democracy allows citizens to confront authority, confidence should be based on knowledge, evidence, and the certainty of numeracy and not conspiracies.

In 2018 the National Council of Teachers of Mathematics (NC) published *Catalyzing Change in High School Mathematics: Initiating Critical Conversations*. This report was followed by publications for elementary and middle school. While the 1989 National Council of Teachers of Mathematics (NCTM) standards promoted mathematics content and processes, those standards also influenced the Common Core Standards for Mathematics (NGA & CCSSO, 2010). The 1989 NCTM and the Common Core State Standards centered on preparation in mathematics for college and careers. The *Catalyzing Change* reports extends and elaborates the purposes of mathematics education to include goals beyond college and careers, including the math students need for quantitative literacy and knowledgeable participation in civic life. The latter includes identifying and interpreting math in contexts such as STEM and other social and cultural systems.

The recognition by these NCTM (2018) reports underscores the credibility of quantitative literacy and its use in everyday contexts. Most, if not all major public issues, ranging from health to the global environment, have associated data, inferences, and predictions that involve mathematics and require critical thinking and reasoned decisions by individuals and societies.

One way to understand the nature of quantitative literacy is to look at implied actions and expressions. Some examples will help clarify the implications of quantitative literacy.

- Understanding the probability of risk.
- Understanding exponential rates of change.
- Understanding the statistics of scientific experiments and engineering designs.
- Understandings of scale, especially of size and speed.
- Understanding the forms, functions, and interpretations of data.

Beyond the context listed above, some skills of quantitative literacy includes the following.

- Data: Using information conveyed in summaries data, i.e., charts and graphs; drawing predictions from data.
- Modeling: Stating explanations, formulating, problems, recognizing interactions in systems and subsystems.
- Statistics: Recognizing the difference between correlation and causation interactions in systems and subsystems.
- Chance: Evaluating risk from current evidence, recognizing the values of random samples.
- Reasoning: Using reasoning to make connections among claims and evidence in explanations and solutions.

## Conclusions

The chapter underscores the critical importance of quantitative literacy for all citizens, highlighting how mathematical understanding, including data interpretation, modeling, statistics, and reasoning, is fundamental to navigating our numerically saturated world. This perspective reframes mathematics as a practical and indispensable component of nearly every field, particularly within science, technology, and engineering. Ultimately, the insights provided in this chapter are crucial for fostering a more integrated and relevant approach to mathematics education within the broader STEM framework, preparing students to critically engage with complex quantitative information.

> **Questions for Discussion:**
>
> ♦ How does the chapter's emphasis on quantitative literacy and its practical applications across scientific, technological, and engineering disciplines influence your perspective on the purpose of mathematics education beyond traditional classrooms?
> ♦ Considering the various components of quantitative literacy discussed, such as data interpretation, modeling, and statistical understanding, what are some effective strategies educators can employ to integrate these skills authentically within interdisciplinary STEM projects?

## References

National Council of Teachers of Mathematics. (2018). *Catalyzing Change in High School Mathematics: Initiating Critical Conversations*. Reston, VA: Author.

National Governors Association & Council of Chief State School Officers (NGA & CCSSO). (2010). *Core State Standards for Mathematics*. Washington, DC: Authors.

Rutherford, F. J., & Ahlgren, A. (1990). *Science for All Americans*. New York: Oxford University Press.

Steen, L. (1997). *Woodrow Wilson National Foundation*. (Name changed to: The Institute for Citizens & Scholars). Princeton, NJ.

Steen, L. (2001). *Mathematics and Democracy: The Case for Quantitative Literacy*. Princeton, NJ: National Council on Education and the Disciplines (NCED).

# Part III

# Exploring Purposes, Policies, and Perspectives for STEM Programs and Practices for STEM Education

# 9

# The Purposes of Education, Including STEM

This chapter reviews historical and contemporary statements about the purposes of education. The priorities proposed for STEM education are relatively recent, e.g., the 1990s, but have connections to ideas with long histories.

> Aim: To provide an historical support for the goals of STEM education and related aims of workforce competences, potential careers in STEM disciplines, and addressing personal and social priorities and issues.
>
> Objectives: Individuals guiding educational change will:
>
> - Be introduced to a definition for STEM literacy,
> - Realize applications for STEM education, and
> - Understand the importance of substantive and sustainable STEM initiatives.
>
> Reflection:
>
> - Suppose you have been asked to propose the aims for a new STEM education initiative.
> - You will have the power to propose, plan, and develop STEM education within a school. The program must be for all students. What aims would you propose? How would you describe the topics, and experiences for students?

DOI: 10.4324/9781003618201-12

**TABLE 9.1** Educational Purpose

> Educational purposes include aims, goals, and rationales. Statement of purpose are universal abstract, and developed for all students and fundamental components of education, e.g., curriculum and assessment. Achieving STEM literacy is an example of a purpose statement.

(Adapted from: Bybee, 1997).

The explorations intent is to have you think about the purposes, content, topics, and experiences that might be appropriate STEM education. Table 9.1 is a brief summary.

Many ideas and ideals have been suggested as aims for education and some have possibly connections to the STEM disciplines, e.g., health, clean air and water, critical thinking, the responsible use of resources.

A brief review of several historical statements about the purposes of education will be insightful. We note this is a sample of educational aims, not a thorough history. As you will see, the priorities we include in STEM education—contexts, competencies, citizenship—have historical precedent. These references refer to general education or, in some cases, science education. Most references predate STEM education; but reasonably include aspects of STEM.

## Examining the Purposes of Education

We begin with an influential report published early in the 20th century—*Commission on the Reorganization of Secondary Education* (1918). The commission described categories that would be the basis for a curriculum for all students, not just those who planned to go to college. The report had seven Cardinal Principles. It stated that the aims of education were: (1) Health, (2) Command of fundamental process (i.e., reading, writing, arithmetic, and oral and written expression), (3) Worthy home membership, (4) Vocation, (5) Citizenship, (6) Worthy use of leisure, and (7) Ethical Character of educational purpose. The larger purpose included development of a full and satisfying life as adult citizens.

The committee also clarified the phrase "basic aspects of living." It identifies the four aspects of living that the committee described: Personal Living; Immediate Personal-Social Relationships; Social-Civic Relationships; and Economic Relationships. The report continued with discussions of the specific science content and the methods that could accommodate the four aspects of living. Please take note of the personal living (health), personal-social,

social-civic and economic themes and ask what current standards and school programs emphasize these goals.

In 1929 Alfred North Whitehead published *The Aims of Education and Other Essays*. In this, he argued against what he called "inert ideas," or ideals, that are received into the mind without being utilized, tested, or combined in new combinations. His recommendations were oriented toward science, and proving the worth of an idea as true by experiment or logic. He claimed that Education is the acquisition of the art of the utilization of knowledge (p. 4). Whitehead's essays hint at our contemporary theme of STEM with titles such as "Technical Education and It's Relation to Science and Literature," "The Mathematical Curriculum," and "The Anatomy of Some Scientific Ideas."

*Science in General Education*, a 1938 publication of the Progressive Education Association, made the following statement about the all-inclusive purpose of secondary education:

> The purpose of general education is to meet the needs of individuals in the basic aspects of living in such way as to promote the fullest possible realization of personal potential and the most effective participation in a democratic society.
>
> (p. 23)

Later, *General Education in a Free Society*, a 1945 Harvard committee report, states that general education is that part of a student's whole education which looks, first of all, to his life as a responsible human being and citizen; similarly, the term special education indicates that part which looks to the students' competence in some occupation (p. 5). In this statement one can identify a distinction between general education and contemporary demands for career education, workforce skills, and 21st-century abilities. Within this context the Harvard committee made this statement about science.

> Science instruction in general education should be characterized mainly by broad integrative elements—the comparison of scientific with other modes of thought, the comparison and contrast of the individual science with its own past and with general human history, and of science with problems of human society.
>
> (p. 155)

Relative to STEM, it seems clear that the Harvard committee would include the nature of science and related disciplines, e.g., technology, engineering, and mathematics. Additionally, it would not be too great a stretch to recognize the crosscutting concepts of NGSS and the application of STEM to contemporary personal and social contexts.

*Policies for Education in American Democracy*, a 1946 report by the Educational Policies Commission, stated that "a domestic way of life is the inclusive purpose of American education" (p. 186). This broad purpose concerns the development of the learner, the human relationships of home, family and community, economic demands, and civic and social duties (pp. 188–189). Science and technology were among the major themes of this report.

## The Emergence of Scientific Literacy

A brief introduction to scientific literacy will clarify and anticipate later discussions of STEM literacy. Originating in the 1950s, the term "scientific literacy" expresses diverse goals ranging from a broad knowledge of science to a particular content of science disciplines.

This term was employed by James B. Conant in 1952 in *General Education in Science*, a volume edited by I. B. Cohen and Fletcher Watson. In the foreword, Conant discusses the need for individual citizens to appraise experts and their advice.

> Such a person might be called an expert on judging experts. Within the field of his experience, he would understand the modern world; in short, he would be well educated in applied science though his factual knowledge of mechanical, electrical, or chemical engineering might be relatively slight. He would be able to communicate intelligently with men who were advancing science and applying it, at least within certain boundaries. The wider his experience, the greater would be his scientific literacy.
>
> (p. xiii)

Paul DeHart Hurd used the term as a major theme for science education. In a 1958 article entitled "Science Literacy: Its Meaning for American Schools," Hurd explained scientific literacy as an understanding of science and its applications to social experience. Science had such a prominent role in society, he argued, that economic, political, and personal issues could not be adequately explained without reference to it. Hurd's article appeared shortly after the 1957 launch of the Russian satellite *Sputnik* and in the earliest phases of major curriculum reform. In this major article, Hurd makes the connection between science and society and then describes the emerging reforms, outlining many of the attributes of curriculum. Because of the historical significance of this article, we quote Hurd's comments at some length:

> There is the problem of building into the science curriculum some depth and quality of understanding. It is essential to select learning materials that are the most fertile in providing opportunities for using methods of science. Further efforts are required to choose learning experiences that have a particular value for development of an appreciation of science as an intellectual achievement, as a procedure for exploration and discovery, and which illustrate the spirit of scientific endeavor.
>
> (pp. 14–15)

Hurd provided a purpose when he unveiled scientific literacy as an understanding of science and its applications to an individual's experience as a citizen. Hurd made clear connections to classroom experiences that provide students with the opportunities to use the methods of science, apply science to social, economic, political and personal issues, and develop an appreciation of science as a human endeavor and an intellectual achievement (Hurd, 1958). Hurd's definition clearly stress the application of scientific knowledge to the situations individuals will encounter as citizens.

Hurd also included the history of science "if it should be presented in its more significant aspect as a major intellectual accomplishment of mankind" (p. 15). Finally, it draws the connection between science and society:

> Today most aspects of human welfare and social progress are influenced in some manner, by scientific and technological innovations. In turn, scientific knowledge established new perspectives for reflection upon social problems. The ramifications of science are such that they can no longer be considered apart from the humanities and the social studies. Modern education has the task of developing an approach to the problems of mankind that considers science, the humanities, and the social studies in a manner so that each discipline will complement the other.
>
> (p. 15)

Although others had employed the term *scientific literacy* before 1958, Paul DeHart Hurd can be credited with enhancing its use among science educators in the 1960s, and also formally introduced the term in contemporary usage in 2000, George DeBoer published a historical review of the term *scientific literacy*. DeBoer suggested a broad conceptualization for scientific literacy, one allowing for variations in curriculum and instruction. The broad goal suggested by DeBoer is generally consistent with earlier definitions—namely, to enhance the public's understanding and appreciation of science. It contains critical insights about scientific literacy—it is about an adult population's level of understanding and appreciation of science, it changes with time and school experiences certainly affect the public's attitudes towards science and their disposition to continue developing their understanding and appreciation of science (DeBoer, 2000).

The Fifth-ninth Yearbook of the National Society for the Study of Education, published in 1960, was titled *Rethinking Science Education*. In it there was an essay which summarized the major purposes included the following categories: Understanding Science, Problem Solving, the Social Aspect of Science, Appreciations, Attitudes, Careers, and Abilities. Each of the respective categories had associated caveats, e.g., teach generalized concepts more than isolated facts. A summary by Paul DeHart Hurd had this insight:

> While the purposes of science education have changed very little in the past twenty-five years, on the other hand there have been changes in the nature of science taught; for example, the sciences have become more unified and have gained an important position in world affairs. These factors suggest the need to re-think the purposes of teaching science in schools.
> (Hurd, 1958, pp. 33–34)

In the *Paideia Proposal: An Educational Manifesto* (1982), Mortimer Adler outlined the goals of basic education as personal growth or self-improvements, preparation for work, and developing citizenship. Adler summarizes the key findings from his study:

> Here then are the three common callings to which our children are destined: to earn a living in an intelligent and responsible fashion, to function as intelligent and responsible citizens, and to make both of these things serve the purpose of leading intelligent lives—to enjoy as fully as possible all the goods that make a human life as good as it can be.
> (Adler, 1982, p. 18)

Adler also points out that schooling is only a part of education. Very importantly, Adler's manifesto underscored the need for *all* students to have a high-quality education that develops basic knowledge, values, and skills enabling them to enter adult life as productive individuals and responsible citizens.

His position was based on pledges of both the Declaration of Independence and the Constitution that each person has a right to life, liberty and the pursuit of happiness. Achieving this goal is based on a mandate of equal educational opportunity for all. At present, we have the same quality—PreK-12 years—of schooling for all. The same quality of schooling for all students is essential in a fully functioning democracy. Here is Adler's position:

> The innermost meaning of social equality is substantially *the same quality of life for all*. That calls for: *the same quality of schooling for all*.
>
> (Adler, 1982, p. 6)

The point we support with this elaboration of Adler's position is that goals and aspirations for STEM education are for *all* students. When Congress passed the Every Student Succeeds Act in 2015, we interpreted that as follows: EVERY student should succeed in STEM education. In *High School* (Boyer, 1983) took a comprehensive and realistic approach to educational reform. One point Boyer makes is central to our proposed goals for STEM education.

> After visiting schools from coast to coast, we are left with the distinct impression that high schools lack a clear and vital mission. They are unable to find common purposes or establish educational priorities that are widely shared. They seem unable to put it all together. The institution is adrift.
>
> (Boyer, 1983, p. 63)

STEM initiatives in schools need not be adrift, but they are. There is no clear and vital mission, no common purpose, and no priorities that are widely shared. We could have a clear and vital mission, common purpose and shared priorities, but they must become components in American education. By developing new goals related to contemporary challenges and STEM, teachers can find the much-needed sense of purpose. Yes, the magnitude of the task is large, but so is the importance of doing the task with an appropriate and accurate vision.

## A New Emphasis for the Science Curriculum

In 1988, F. James Rutherford and Andrew Ahlgren published a chapter entitled "Rethinking the Science Curriculum" in the yearbook of the Association for Supervision and Curriculum Development (ASCD). This chapter presented an innovative combination of science, technology (including engineering), and mathematics. The chapter was an initial summary of Project 2061: Education for a Changing Future, which had been launched in 1985 by the American Association for the Advancement of Science (AAAS) with financial support from the Carnegie Corporation of New York and the Andrew W. Mellon Foundation.

Project 2061 is a long-term effort by the scientific community to completely rethink the purposes of school science, including mathematics and technology. The first task of project was to answer the question: What science, mathematics, and technology should all students have learned by the time they complete their elementary and secondary education?

As Project 2061 committees approached the mission of rethinking the purposes of science education, they were guided by a series of categories and questions such as the following:

- *Strategy*. How can the science curriculum for all students be specified in a way that will encourage building a new and unique set of innovations?
- *Scope*. What sciences should "school science" comprise? Mathematics as a part of science? Computer and information sciences?
- *Emphasis*. Which aspects of science should the science curriculum concentrate on? Accumulated knowledge: History? Methods of inquiry and problem solving? Science in human affairs?
- *Selection Criteria*. What educational purposes should be used to guide the selection of the content of the school science? The needs of citizens? The needs of the country? Preparation for the workplace?

Because this chapter presents guides for your understanding educational purposes for STEM we have slightly adapted the list originally described in the chapter by Rutherford and Ahlgren (Table 9.2).

Rutheford and Ahlgren went on to present results from Project 2061 committees in *Science for All Americans* (1990). The book is about scientific literacy. The book includes broad and insightful discussions of STEM disciplines and implications for reform of school programs and teaching practices.

## Purposes for STEM Education

Based on the sample historical statements about the purposes of education in general, and science education in particular, we propose that the larger sense of advancing STEM education should center on three complementary purposes:

**TABLE 9.2** Educational Purpose

| Strategies |
|---|
| **Principle 1**: To build an effective STEM curriculum, it is first necessary to identify what students should end up knowing.<br>**Principle 2**: The learning goals for particular student populations (vocational, college preparatory, general) and for students of different interests and ability, should build on those set for *all* students.<br>**Principle 3**: In order to reduce the tendency to redistribute all of the existing STEM curriculum content into new categories, learning goals should be expressed conceptually rather than as a list of topic headings.<br>**Principle 4**: A statement of learning outcomes in STEM should be accompanied by comments on teaching practices that are especially important for realizing those out comes. |
| **Scope** |
| **Principle 5**: The content of the school STEM curriculum should be relevant to but not necessarily exhaustively representative of) the full spectrum of the STEM disciplines.<br>**Principle 6**: School STEM learning goals should incorporate mathematics content when mathematics is conceptually or historically linked to the recommended science, technology, and engineering concepts, but mathematizing STEM should be avoided when, as is often the case, it makes learning the other disciplines substantially more difficult.<br>**Principle 7**: The STEM curriculum should include content related to all four disciplines.<br>**Principle 8**: STEM education goals should be defined in a way that encourages frequent curricular crossover between the STEM and the humanities. |
| **Emphasis** |
| **Principle 9**: The STEM curriculum should deal with all of the STEM disciplines.<br>**Principle 10**: The STEM curriculum should include content that deals with the role of STEM in other human affairs. |
| **Criteria** |
| **Principle 11**: The selection of the content of school STEM should be based on explicitly stated educational criteria. |

(Adapted for STEM from: Rutherford & Ahlgren, 1988).

- Achieving higher levels of STEM literacy for all citizens,
- Developing a deep technical workforce—one that meets 21$^{st}$-century needs, and
- Attaining an advanced research and development workforce with diverse individuals in the professions.

To be more specific, STEM literacy includes the conceptual understandings and procedural skills and abilities needed for all individuals to address STEM-related personal, social, and global issues. For example, STEM education would involve the basic concepts and processes of STEM disciplines and include appropriate content from state standards. Education for STEM literacy would address the following goals: Gain definitions for STEM literacy,

- Acquire scientific, technological, engineering and mathematical knowledge and use that knowledge to competently identify issues, acquire new knowledge, and apply the knowledge to STEM-related issues.
- Understand the characteristic features of STEM disciplines as forms of human endeavors that include the processes of inquiry, design, and analysis.
- Recognize how STEM disciplines contribute to our material, intellectual, and cultural world.
- Encourage in STEM-related personal and social issues as concerned, effective and constructive citizens.

We recommend an authentic STEM literacy, one that includes, but extends beyond, reading writing, and discussion. While we certainly recognize the importance of these basics, we expand the use of authentic to include: (1) life situations such as public health, resources, environment, and hazards that are directly related to STEM; and (2) processes that require students to make sense of the life situations by emphasizing a model of claim–evidence–reason in their discussions, reports, and presentations.

## Conclusions

The chapter emphasizes the importance of aligning educational goals with the practical applications of STEM, including workforce competencies, career opportunities, and addressing personal and societal issues. Ultimately, understanding these foundational purposes is crucial for developing substantive and sustainable STEM initiatives that effectively prepare all students for the challenges and opportunities of the future. It highlights those statements of purpose, such as achieving STEM literacy, are fundamental and universal components that guide curriculum and assessment.

> **Question for Discussion:**
>
> ♦ How would you express the purposes of STEM education for your colleagues? Administrators? State Board of Education?

## References

Adler, M. (1982). *The Paideia Proposal: An Educational Manifesto*. New York: Colier M., San Francisco, CA: Jossey-Bass Publishers.

Boyer, E. (1983). *Nigh School: A Report on Secondary Education in America*. New York: Harper & Row Publishers.

Bybee, R. W. (1997). *Achieving Scientific Literacy: From Purposes to Practices*. Portsmouth, NH: Heinemann Publishing.

Cohen, I. B., & Watson, F. G. (1952). *General Education in Science*. Cambridge, MA: Harvard University Press.

Commission on the Reorganization of Secondary Education. (1918). *Cardinal Principles of Secondary Education*. Washington, DC: Bureau of Education, Bulletin No. 35.

DeBoer, G. E. (2000). Scientific literacy: Another look at its historical and contemporary meanings and its relationship to science education reform. *Journal of Research in Science Teaching*, Vol. 37(6): pp. 582–601.

Education Policies Commission. (1946). *Policies for Education in American Democracy*. Washington, DC: National Education Association.

Harvard Committee. (1945). *General Education in a Free Society*. Cambridge, MA: Harvard University Press.

Hurd, P. D. (1958). Science literacy: It's meaning for American Schools. *Educational Leadership*, Vol. 16: pp. 13–16.

National Society for the Study of Education. (1960). *Rethinking Science Education*. Barnard, J. Darell (Chair of Committee). Chicago, IL: The University of Chicago Press.

Progressive Education Association. (1938). *Science in General Education*. New York: Appleton-Century Crofts.

Rutherford, F. J., & Ahlgren, A. (1988). Rethinking the science curriculum. In Brandt, R. (Ed.). *Content of the Curriculum 1988 ASDC Yearbook* (pp. 75–90). Alexandra, VA: Association for Supervision and Curriculum Development (ASCD).

# 10

# Policies for STEM Education, Including Standards

This chapter review presents a central question, one that identifies policies for STEM education programs and practices.

> Aim: To describe policies that will guide decisions for STEM initiatives in curriculum, instruction, assessment, and teachers' professional learning.
>
> Objectives: Individuals providing leadership for education will:
>
> - Broaden and deepen their understanding of educational policies,
> - Identify topics for STEM programs,
> - Expand their perspectives for advancing STEM education, and
> - Recognize opportunities for advancing STEM literacy, a technical workforce, and careers.
>
> Reflections:
>
> - Suppose you have the idea of introducing a STEM initiative in your educational system. For this reflection you can imagine the educational system is your state, district, school, or classroom. You decided the initiative should emphasize STEM literacy.
> - When you present the idea to your administrator she responded—"I like the idea of STEM, what I need is a plan for something in particular to be done and how it will be completed."

> - Working with a colleague, prepare a brief proposal that responds to the administrator's response to the administrator's request.
> - In the simplest form, the reflection engaged your thinking in some specific content and a plan for designing and developing selected content. The administrator's request had you translate the purpose of STEM into specific content and a manner of doing something to help others, i.e., students learning the content.

The *Next Generation Science Standards* (NGSS Lead States, 2013a) exemplifies contemporary policies. They include specific content and imply some organization, experiences, and strategies that will enhance students' learning. Educational policies can address or imply curriculum, instruction, and assessment for teaching different grades and content. They may also inform and regulate decisions about the actual design and development of programs.

Policies would, for example, help answer questions about the content and strategies to achieve STEM literacy. Policies are not as abstract as purposes, and they give direction; but they are not as concrete as actual curriculum materials and teaching strategies. See Table 10.1 for a summary statement of educational policies as we are using the terms.

## Proposed Policies for STEM Education

This chapter continues with recommendations of policies that will advance STEM education. Using the categories introduced in the prior chapter on purposes here we introduce content and suggestions for addressing the means of incorporating the content in the design of instructional experiences. Three categories comprise the larger purposes of STEM education and its

**TABLE 10.1** Educational Policies

| |
|---|
| Educational policies are specific statement of purposes and may take the form of standards, benchmarks, state frameworks, school district syllabi, and curriculum designs. Policy statements are concrete translations of the purposes and apply to educational components such as disciplines, grade levels, curriculum, instruction, and assessments. Policies may also include knowledge, skills, and attitudes. *Generation Science Standards*, (NGSS/Lead States, 2013b), is an example of educational policies. |

(Adapted from: Bybee, 1997).

contribution to society. A question sets the stage for the discussion—How can STEM education contribute to three goals:

- Developing a STEM-literate society,
- Proposing a deep technical workforce for the 21st century, and
- Advancing a research and development workforce focused on innovation?

## A STEM-literate Society

How can educators advance STEM literacy? The first thing to understand is that a 21st-century perspective requires students as future adult citizens to apply knowledge of the STEM disciplines to meaningful life situations. Table 10.2 is a definition of STEM literacy and identifies differences between STEM literacy and traditional views of curriculum based on the respective STEM disciplines.

Clearly STEM literacy includes the basic science, technology, engineering, and mathematics concepts and processes, but it must go beyond this traditional discipline-bound view. Rather, it should center on education that consists of the general education of all citizens. Although understanding foundational subject matter in the sciences, technology, engineering, and mathematics is essential, one must consider the use and application of that knowledge, not just the acquisition of knowledge as the learning outcome.

The 21st-century STEM view requires students as adult citizens to apply knowledge from the STEM disciplines to life situations. Table 10.3 displays examples of policies for personal and social STEM-related contexts.

**TABLE 10.2** A Definition of STEM Literacy

| STEM literacy refers to an individual's |
|---|
| • knowledge, attitudes, and skills to identify questions and problems in life situations, to explain the natural and designed world, and to draw evidence-based conclusions about STEM-related issues, <br> • understanding of the characteristic features of STEM disciplines as forms of human knowledge, inquiry, and design, <br> • awareness of how STEM disciplines shape our material, intellectual, and cultural environments, and <br> • willingness to engage in STEM-related issues and with the ideas of science, technology, engineering, and mathematics as a constructive, sensible, and reflective citizen. |

(Adapted from: Bybee et al., 2009; OECD, 2006).

**TABLE 10.3** STEM Education and 21st-century Contexts

| Global, national, and local issues | Health maintenance and disease prevention<br>Energy efficiency<br>Environmental quality<br>Natural hazards<br>Natural resource use<br>Understanding of STEM disciplines |
|---|---|
| Educational theme | A STEM-literate society |
| Advancing the goals of STEM education | Address 21st-century grand challenges in appropriate programs, courses, and classes<br>Provide opportunities for the applications of knowledge and skills to STEM-related issues<br>Include scientific, engineering, design, and mathematical practices |

There should be a clear distinction between an education that prepares for future study of STEM disciplines, for example, and an education that contributes to students' growth into literate adults. As literate adults, individuals should be competent to understand STEM-related issues, recognize scientific from nonscientific explanations, make reasonable arguments based on evidence, and, very importantly, fulfill civic duties at the local, national, and global levels.

To conclude, for those interested in developing STEM-literate citizens, students should have experiences where they confront appropriate socioscientific issues and problems within meaningful contexts. With the centrality of science, technology, engineering, and mathematics to contemporary life, full participation in society requires that all adults, including those aspiring to careers as scientists, engineers, and mathematicians, be STEM-literate.

## A Deep Technical Workforce

This policy includes all students, not just those destined for careers in science, technology, engineering, and mathematics. The skills described here apply to a broad range of 21st-century careers. Activities in science, technology, engineering, and mathematics lessons and courses provide many opportunities to develop the skills needed for a deep technical workforce. Table 10.4 summarizes policies for this aim.

Many reports (e.g., National Research Council, 2010) have references to developing capacities such as intellectual skills, cognitive abilities, scientific reasoning, and problem solving—in short, those needed to create a deep

**TABLE 10.4** STEM Education and 21st-Century Skills

| National issue | Knowledge economy |
|---|---|
| Education theme | A deep technical workforce |
| Advancing the goals of STEM education | Develop students 21st-century skills and abilities:<br>♦ Adaptability<br>♦ Complex communication<br>♦ Nonroutine problem solving<br>♦ Self-management/self-development<br>Systems thinking |

(Adapted from *Exploring the Intersection of Science Education and 21st Century Skills* [NRC, 2010]).

technical workforce. Such abilities should be fundamental as one considers STEM programs, teacher education, and professional development. Developing the mental processes of scientific inquiry and engineering design, for example, is the direct outcome of engaging students in appropriate experiences that require the practice and application of such cognitive abilities. STEM educators know how to design programs that provide students opportunities to achieve these aims while developing a deep and rich understanding of basic scientific, technological, engineering, and mathematical ideas.

### Careers in Advanced Research and Development

Pipeline issues continue, especially for computer scientists, environmental scientists, engineers, and health professionals. In addition, increasing the diversity of individuals in STEM careers remains a central goal that can be addressed in STEM programs. STEM education can contribute to the recruitment and retention of individuals into STEM-related careers. Such careers will be the basis for innovations needed for a quality environment, prosperous economy, and healthy society. Table 10.5 summarizes policies for STEM education.

In the 20th century, federal investment in scientific and technological research made substantial innovations that contributed to better health, improved communications, and what has to be counted among the greatest technological and engineering accomplishments in human history—sending men to the Moon and bringing them back safely. Many of these innovations grew out of the physical sciences. The discoveries around DNA by Frances Crick and James Watson, as well as Maurice Wilkins and Rosalind Franklin, in the 1950s influenced many innovations in molecular and cellular biology.

**TABLE 10.5** STEM Education and Careers

| National issue | Innovation |
|---|---|
| Educational theme | An advanced research and development workforce |
| Advancing the goals of STEM education | Focus on STEM Careers to<br>♦ Increase the number and diversity of students in STEM professions,<br>♦ Recruit top students to STEM professions, and<br>♦ Keep individuals in STEM careers. |

Advancements in STEM disciplines have continually accounted for innovations and increases in the US gross domestic product (GDP), an indicator of economic productivity. It is also the case that solutions to many of our local, national, and global challenges will result from advances in STEM disciplines. For example, responses to health, energy, environmental quality, natural hazards, and the use of natural resources. All of these fields depend on a continued flow of individuals in a professional pipeline from K-12 schools to colleges and universities and, in most cases, to graduate programs. Federal investment in basic research plays the major role in innovation. K-12 STEM programs should recognize this and be a part of students' education.

## State Policies for Science Education: Beneficial Resources for STEM

At some point in your consideration of STEM education you likely thought about science standards for your state and their relationship to possible STEM initiatives. As it turns out, a majority of states have adopted new state standards for science, and many of those standards include technology and engineering. The inclusion of technology and engineering in state standards was greatly enhanced by the publication of *A Framework for K-12 Science Education: Practices, Crosscutting Concepts, and Core Ideas* (NRC, 2012). This Framework was designed to be the foundation for new science standards—*Next Generation Science Standards* (NGSS/Lead States, 2013b). In Table 10.6, you will recognize traditional content categories for science education, i.e., Core Ideas for Physical, Life, and Earth and Space Sciences. Other dimensions of the Framework include "Science and Engineering Practices" and "Crosscutting Concepts." .

**TABLE 10.6** Table of Content– *A Framework for K-12 Science Education: Practices, Crosscutting Concepts, and Core Ideas* (NAS, 2012)

| Table of Contents |
|---|
| Foreword<br>Acknowledgements<br>Summary |
| PART I: A Vision for K-12 Science Education<br>  1 A New Conceptual Framework<br>  2 Guiding Assumptions and Organization of the Framework |
| PART II: Dimensions of the Framework<br>  3 Dimension 1: Scientific and Engineering Practices<br>  4 Dimension 2: Crosscutting Concepts<br>  5 Dimension 3: Disciplinary Core Ideas—Physical Sciences<br>  6 Dimension 3: Disciplinary Core Ideas—Life Sciences<br>  7 Dimension 3: Disciplinary Core Ideas—Earth and Space Sciences<br>  8 Dimension 3: Disciplinary Core Ideas—Engineering, Technology, and Applications of Science |
| PART III: Realizing the Vision<br>  9 Integrate the Three Dimensions<br>  10 Implementation: Curriculum, Instruction, Teacher Development, and Assessment<br>  11 Equity and Diversity in Science and Engineering Education<br>  12 Guidance for Standards Developers<br>Looking Toward the Future: Research and Development to Inform K-12 |

(Adapted from: NRC, 2012).

## Conclusion

STEM education cannot take full responsibility for achieving the knowledge values, skills and sensibilities of STEM-literate adult citizens. It can, however, contribute to this aim through the policies described in this chapter. To conclude: what policies should guide STEM education in the 21st century? We responded with one major purpose—STEM-literate citizenship, and two supporting goals, a deep technical workforce and an advanced research and development workforce focused on innovation. Answering the question that heads this paragraph and thinking about the possibilities for STEM education programs and practices gave insights into contexts and competencies as meaningful and useful ways to help students develop their knowledge, values, skills, and sensibilities relative to STEM.

**Questions for Discussion:**

- What are the essential points of policies for contemporary STEM education?
- What is your response to the definition of STEM literacy?
- What are the 21st-century skills described in this chapter, and how could you imagine their development in the context of STEM education programs and practices?
- Innovation was described as a national issue. Assuming it is, what could STEM education do to encourage innovation?

## References

Bybee, R. W. (1997). *Achieving Scientific Literacy: From Purposes to Practices*. Portsmouth, NH: Heinemann.

Bybee, R.W., McCrae, B., & Laurie, R. (2009). PISA 2006: An Assessment of Scientific Literacy. *Journal of Research in Science Teaching*, 46(8), 865–886.

National Research Council (NRC). (2010). *Exploring the Intersection Science Education and 21st Century Skills*. Washington, DC: The National Academies Press.

National Research Council. (2012). *A Framework for K-12 Science Education: Practices, Crosscutting Concepts, and Core Ideas*. Washington, DC: The National Academies Press.

NGSS Lead States. (2013a). *Next Generation Science Standards: For States, By States*. Vol 1: *The Standards-Arranged by Disciplinary Core Ideas and by Topics*. Washington, DC: The National Academies Press.

NGSS Lead States. (2013b). *Next Generation Science Standards: For States, By States. Vol 2: Appendixes*. Washington, DC: The National Academies Press.

Organisation for Economic Co-operation and Development (OECD). (2006). *Assessing Scientific, Reading and Mathematical Literacy: A Framework for PISA 2006*. Paris, France: OECD Publishing.

# 11

# STEM Programs, Including Curriculum and Assessment

This chapter's primary themes include ways to create a STEM program that works with Standards and aligns with modern research on learning and assessment. Recommendations in the chapter focus on beginning instructional design with the end goals for learning and transfer.

> Aim: To focus and prioritize learning, content, skills, and practices appropriately
>
> Objectives: Individuals and professional learning teams considering designing or evaluating STEM experiences will:
>
> ♦ Make connections between goals, standards, transfer, and assessments.
> ♦ Bridge an effective framework for instructional design with current practices.
>
> Reflection Questions:
>
> ♦ What are the essential features you consider when evaluating instructional materials for STEM education?
> ♦ How do the current assessments align with proposed STEM learning goals?

As a brief reminder, the term programs refers to the actual instructional materials, for example unit of activities, textbooks, on-line materials, and competitions. In the context of this book, programs would be the STEM instructional materials that are used in classroom lessons' course for schools.

To avoid the persistent issue of curricula that are "a mile wide and an inch deep" (Schmidt, 2004, experts recommend structuring instructional materials on a smaller number of conceptually significant, transferable ideas. This approach, championed by curriculum theorists such as Wiggins and McTighe (2005, 2011) and Erickson (2020), encourages educators to move beyond exhaustive content coverage. Instead, they should prioritize cultivating deeper understanding by focusing on regional, national, or global issues and problems through the consideration of essential concepts that transcend specific subjects and contexts.

By streamlining program content, educators can create space for students to engage in active processes essential for developing critical thinking, problem-solving skills, and conceptual understanding. This shift allows for a more intentional focus on connecting ideas, fostering interdisciplinary learning, and applying knowledge to meaningful contexts. While this vision for education is elegant in its design, it requires significant changes in traditional teaching practices and a commitment to rethinking program design to better prepare students for a complex, rapidly changing world.

## Bridging Standards and Programs in STEM Education

One of the challenges in STEM education is the misconception that Standards are equivalent to curriculum. Standards outline the content and processes students should know and be able to do; they do not dictate how to teach or structure learning experiences. This distinction is crucial because it underscores the need for teachers and curriculum designers to create coherent pathways for students, ensuring that learning is meaningful, and fosters long-term understanding.

Using Understanding by Design (UbD) as a framework to develop STEM instructional materials is particularly beneficial (Wiggins and McTighe, 2005, 2011). UbD aligns well with the intentions of modern cognitive science research, which emphasizes deep conceptual understanding and the ability to apply knowledge across different contexts (Bransford, Brown, & Cocking, 2000; McTighe & Silver, 2020). By focusing on big ideas rather than isolated facts, UbD supports a STEM-oriented mindset—one that encourages integration across science, technology, engineering, and mathematics rather than treating each domain as a separate subject.

## Why Transfer of Learning Matters in STEM

One key component of UbD, and high-quality STEM education in general, is the concept of transferring the ability to take what is learned in one context and apply it to another. Setting high goals for students to develop and transfer those abilities is a hallmark of cognitive science research where, in the long run, students should be able to do something with their learning (Bransford, Brown, & Cocking, 2000). Transfer is especially relevant in STEM fields, where students must not only acquire knowledge but also use it creatively, flexibly, and fluently to solve meaningful problems.

The National Academies report *Rising Above the Gathering Storm: Energizing and Employing America for a Brighter Future* (2007) recommended that students will need contemporary abilities such as adaptability, complex communications, social skills, nonroutine problem solving, self-management, and systems thinking to compete in the 21st century. Recognizing that STEM curricula incorporate group activities, laboratory investigations, and projects, they afford the opportunity for students to develop these essential 21st-century skills and prepare them to become citizens who are better able to make decisions about personal health, energy efficiency, environmental quality, resource use, and national security. Indeed, the competencies that citizens need to understand and address such issues, from the personal to global perspectives, are clearly linked to knowledge in the STEM disciplines.

In the STEM workforce, professionals constantly analyze data, apply logical reasoning, and integrate discipline-specific knowledge to innovate and develop new technologies, solve engineering challenges, and make informed decisions based on scientific principles. Teaching for transfer means ensuring that students move beyond rote memorization and develop habits of mind that allow them to approach complex problems with confidence.

## The Role of Foundational Skills in STEM Education

Focusing on understanding and transfer does not mean ignoring fundamental skills or factual knowledge. In STEM, foundational knowledge is essential—students must have a grasp of key concepts and skills before they can apply them. However, educators should view foundational knowledge as the starting point (the floor), not the end point (the ceiling) of learning. For example, a student learning about Newton's Laws of Motion should not only understand the laws but also be able to apply them in engineering challenges, such as designing a bridge or testing the efficiency of different vehicle designs. A student working with coding and robotics should not only learn basic programming commands but also use them creatively to automate processes, design solutions, or model authentic scenarios. This approach ensures that students develop both depth and flexibility in their learning—preparing them for future STEM-related situations where they will need to adapt to new challenges and innovations.

By using processes like UbD to backward-design STEM learning experiences, educators can ensure that instruction is goal-oriented, conceptually rich, and transferable beyond the classroom. This approach not only can accommodate modern standards but also nurtures STEM-literate students who are capable of transferring concepts across disciplines, applying knowledge in novel situations, and contributing to a rapidly evolving workforce. Ultimately, the goal of STEM education is not just to teach science, technology, engineering, and mathematics as separate subjects but to cultivate the ability to integrate, innovate, and solve problems—skills that are essential for the 21st-century workforce and citizens in general.

## The Three Stages of Backward Design in STEM Education

The **UbD framework** provides a structured approach to planning STEM programs that ensures coherence, clarity, and alignment. It operates on the principle that **teaching is a means to an end**—not just the transmission of facts but the facilitation of deep, transferable understanding. The first step in backward design is defining clear learning outcomes (Wiggins & McTighe, 2005, 2011). This involves establishing the essential understandings that students should take away from the STEM program. Once the desired learning outcomes are established, the next step is determining the appropriate evidence that demonstrates student understand the learning outcomes. This goes beyond traditional tests and quizzes to incorporate authentic assessments that require students to apply their learning. The key here is ensuring that assessments measure deep understanding, not just memorization of facts. If students can explain, apply, and justify their reasoning using evidence, they are demonstrating true mastery of the concept. Only after establishing the "what" (i.e., learning outcomes, desired results) and the "did they learn?" (i.e., acceptable evidence of achievement) do educators plan the sequence of experiences.

### Stage 1: Identifying Desired Results in STEM Education
The first stage of UbD is crucial because it sets the foundation for everything that follows. It requires educators to clarify instructional priorities by

identifying what students should know, understand, and be able to do by the end of a unit, for example. In STEM education, this means designing units based on phenomena and authentic problems that encourage inquiry and application.

A well-designed STEM unit aligns with Transfer Goals, ensuring that students can take their learning beyond the classroom. These goals reflect how students will use their knowledge in future academic, professional, and everyday contexts. Educators first determine the overarching learning goals based on national and state standards. Each STEM discipline has standards that provide a foundation for curriculum planning:

- Science: Next *Generation Science Standards* (NGSS) (2013)
- Technology: *International Society for Technology in Education* (ISTE) (2000)
- Engineering: *NGSS Engineering Practices* (2013)
- Mathematics: *Common Core State Standards* (CCSS) (2010)

These standards define the content that students should learn and ensure that instruction is aligned with the latest advancements in STEM education.

UbD emphasizes that students should acquire both content knowledge and develop deep conceptual understanding as well as the ability to apply their learning to new contexts. This is where Big Ideas and Transfer Goals come into play.

- Big Ideas: Fundamental, enduring understandings that students should retain long after instruction ends (Wiggins and McTighe, 2011).
- Transfer Goals: The ability to apply learning in new, unpredictable situations beyond the classroom (McTighe & Silver, 2020).

For a unit on severe weather and climate change, the Big Ideas and Transfer Goals should be coordinated and might look like those in Table 11.1.

Essential Questions are open-ended thought-provoking questions that encourage critical thinking and inquiry. They help guide student investigations and make learning more meaningful by engagingly framing concepts. In the severe weather unit, for example, some Essential Questions might include those in Table 11.2.

The questions in Table 11.2 encourage students to think in terms of connections among STEM disciplines.

Once the big ideas and essential questions are established, educators outline key understandings that students should develop. These understandings

**TABLE 11.1** Examples of Learning Outcomes for a STEM Program on Climate Change and Weather

| Representative Big Ideas: |
|---|
| ♦ Human activities, such as burning fossil fuels, influence the Earth's climate and contribute to extreme weather events.<br>♦ Advancements in technology and engineering contribute to scientists tracking, predicting, and mitigating the effects of severe weather.<br>♦ Mathematical models advance scientists' analysis of climate data and predictions of future weather patterns. |
| **Representative Transfer Goals:** |
| ♦ Students will analyze real-time weather data to make predictions about upcoming storm systems.<br>♦ Students will be able to evaluate how different climate policies impact severe weather trends.<br>♦ Students will use engineering design principles to develop solutions for reducing the impact of climate change. |

**TABLE 11.2** Essential Questions for a STEM Program on Severe Weather

| Representative Essential Questions: |
|---|
| ♦ Science: How does climate change influence the frequency and intensity of severe weather events?<br>♦ Technology: How do technological advancements improve our ability to predict and respond to severe weather?<br>♦ Engineering: What role do engineers play in designing infrastructure that can withstand extreme weather?<br>♦ Mathematics: How do scientists use mathematical models to predict future climate trends? |

ensure that students are actively making sense of their learning rather than simply recalling information.

For the severe weather and climate change unit, the understanding could include those in Table 11.3.

These understanding statements ensure that students develop a comprehensive, interdisciplinary perspective that connects science, technology, engineering, and mathematics to real-world applications. In addition, this process illustrates the connection of standards to big ideas.

Finally, the acquisition goals refer to the specific knowledge and skills that serve as building blocks for understanding. Acquisition goals help students

**TABLE 11.3** Representative Understanding for a STEM Unit

| Representative Understandings |
|---|
| ♦ Science: The release of greenhouse gases contributes to climate change, leading to more frequent and intense weather events (NGSS, 2013).<br>♦ Technology: Advanced radar and satellite technology allow meteorologists to track storms and improve disaster preparedness (ISTE, 2000).<br>♦ Engineering: Engineers develop solutions to mitigate severe weather impacts, such as flood barriers and heat-resistant building materials (NGSS, 2013).<br>♦ Mathematics: Climate models use statistical analysis and data trends to predict future weather patterns (CCSS, 2010). |

**TABLE 11.4** Representative Acquisition Goals for STEM Literacy

| Representative Acquisition Goals: |
|---|
| ♦ Define greenhouse gases and explain their role in the Earth's climate system.<br>♦ Technology: Identify types of meteorological technology (e.g., Doppler radar, weather satellites, computer models).<br>♦ Engineering: Identify and describe engineering solutions designed to reduce severe weather impacts (e.g., seawalls, green infrastructure, permeable pavement).<br>♦ Mathematics: Analyze historical climate data using basic statistical measures (mean, median, mode, variability). |

engage with the key understandings and so they can develop higher levels of STEM literacy (see Table 11.4).

Going through the process discussed in Stage 1 of UbD ensures that STEM instructional materials are purposeful and goal-driven rather than a collection of disconnected activities. It allows educators to ensure curriculum alignment with standards that focus on developing deep conceptual understanding. When Stage 1 is thoughtfully developed, the rest of the unit (Stages 2 and 3) naturally follows, leading to engaging, hands-on learning experiences that prepare students for real-world STEM challenges.

### Stage 2: Determining Acceptable Evidence of learning STEM Programs

Once learning goals have been clearly defined in Stage 1, educators must consider what counts as evidence of learning and how they will assess whether students have met those goals. Stage 2 of UbD encourages teachers to think like assessors first—before planning instruction—to ensure that assessments effectively measure both content mastery and the ability to apply knowledge in new contexts.

**TABLE 11.5** Stage 1 of the UbD Unit STEM Template

| Stage 1 Desired Results | | |
|---|---|---|
| Big Ideas | Transfer | |
| | Students will be able to independently use their learning to.... | |
| | Meaning | |
| | Understandings<br>Students will understand that... | Essential Questions<br>Students will keep considering.... |
| | Acquisition | |
| | Students will know.... | Students will be skilled at... |

This stage is particularly critical in STEM education, where students must go beyond recalling facts and instead analyze data, design experiments, build models, and apply their understanding to solve authentic problems. Traditional assessments, quizzes, tests, and skill checks are useful for measuring basic knowledge and procedural fluency. However, they do not fully capture conceptual understanding or the ability to apply learning. Therefore, UbD emphasizes performance assessments, which require students to demonstrate their knowledge in meaningful ways (Wiggins & McTighe, 2005, 2011). Performance assessments ask students to apply their learning to new situations, construct explanations, and justify their reasoning using evidence-based claims. These tasks should be set in actual situations and authentic contexts, ensuring that students are engaged in meaningful applications of STEM knowledge.

Following the examples in Stage 1 for severe weather and climate change, teachers might create a performance event where students write an evidence-based explanation about how human activity influences weather events. In this task, students would be asked to do more than just recall information, but actively engage in using the STEM disciplines to analyze, model, and reason using the ideas from above related to the answers to the essential questions. A fundamental principle of Stage 2 is the idea that if the goal of education is to equip students to transfer their learning to new situations, then assessments should reflect this goal. This means prioritizing that students are engaging in the actual work of scientists, technologists, engineers, and mathematicians. We have provided a template to organize evaluation criteria and performance assessments in Table 11.5.

## Stage 3: Plan for Learning Experiences and Instruction in a STEM Program

Stage 3 of UbD is where day-to-day instruction takes shape. This stage ensures that lessons, instructional strategies, and learning experiences are purposefully designed to support the learning goals (Stage 1) and align with assessment evidence (Stage 2).

A well-structured education program is not just about covering content—it is about engaging authentic applications of knowledge. By focusing on evidence-based reasoning, assessments ensure students in active learning, where they construct meaning through exploration and application.

A central idea in UbD is that understanding cannot simply be delivered—students must construct their meaning, i.e., make sense, through inquiry, investigation, and problem solving. This concept is particularly important in STEM education, where students must:

- Engage with authentic phenomena, problems, and life situations,
- Make sense of data and evidence,
- Use engineering and mathematical thinking to develop solutions, and
- Apply technology and computational tools to analyze and solve the challenge.

Rather than starting with direct instruction, an UbD-aligned Stage 3 learning plan would engage students in meaning-making activities:

- Engagement in STEM phenomena, problems, and issues that may be local or global.
- Conduct and perform investigations including exploration and library research.
- Identify patterns in the data and discuss what they notice as evidence for understanding.
- Work in teams or individually to construct explanations.
- Generate additional questions that need explanations and further elaborations.
- Reflect on learning and developing understanding.
- Students put together components needed to address the performance assessment.

By using these research-based practices, students earn their understanding rather than passively receiving information. By structuring Stage 3 thoughtfully, STEM educators create engaging, hands-on, and authentic learning environments that prepare students to think critically, solve problems, and apply their knowledge beyond the classroom.

## Conclusions

The chapter advocates for an instructional design approach that prioritizes end goals for learning and transfer, moving beyond superficial coverage to foster deeper understanding. It addresses the pervasive challenge of curricula that are "a mile wide and an inch deep" by emphasizing the structuring of materials around conceptually significant and transferable ideas. Ultimately, this chapter provides a foundational framework for educators to bridge theoretical understandings of effective instructional design with practical approaches to creating coherent and impactful STEM programs and assessments that truly serve student learning.

---

**Questions for Discussion:**

- ♦ Chapter 11 emphasizes the importance of starting instructional design with "end goals for learning and transfer." How can educators effectively integrate this principle into their STEM program development to ensure that curriculum and assessment truly foster deep understanding and transferable skills, rather than a "mile wide and an inch deep" approach?
- ♦ The chapter highlights the need for STEM programs to align with both standards and modern research on learning and assessment. What are the most significant challenges schools might face in achieving this alignment, particularly when designing or evaluating STEM instructional materials and assessments?

---

## References

Bransford, J., Brown, A., & Cocking, R. (2000). *How People Learn: Brain, Mind, Experience, and School*. Washington, DC: National Academies Press.

Erickson, H. L. (2020). *Concept-Based Curriculum and Instruction for the Thinking Classroom*. Thousand Oaks, CA: Corwin Press.

International Society for Technology in Education. (2000). *National Educational Technology Standards (NETS)*. Eugene, OR: Author.

McTighe, J., & Silver, H. (2020). *Teaching for Deeper Learning: Tools to Engage Students in Meaning Making*. Alexandria, VA: ASCD.

National Governors Association Center for Best Practices & Council of Chief State School Officers. (2010). *Common Core State Standards*. Authors.

NGSS Lead States. (2013). *Next Generation Science Standards: For States, by States*. National Academies Press. https://www.nextgenscience.org/next-generation-science-standards

Schmidt, W. (2004). *From Papers and Presentations, Mathematics and Science Initiative*. U.S. Department of Education. https://www.ed.gov/print/rschstat/research/progs/mathscience/schmidt.html

Wiggins, J., & McTighe, J. (2005). *Understanding by Design*: Expanded 2nd Edition. Alexandria, VA: ASCD.

Wiggins, J., & McTighe, J. (2011). *Understanding by Design Guide to Creating High Quality Units*. Alexandria, VA: ASCD.

# 12

# STEM Practices

## Using Effective Instructional Sequences

This chapter's primary themes include comparing ways to sequence STEM instructional activities, thus helping students make sense of their world. Recommendations in the chapter synthesize contemporary learning theory and classroom instructional models.

> Aim: To clarify the theme of sensemaking and the connections to STEM education.
>
> Objectives: Individuals and professional learning teams considering implementation of STEM education will:
>
> - Make connections with the activities used to teach and an order for sequencing them to leverage the highest learning possible.
> - Bridge the theories of learning and instructional sequences and strategies.
>
> Reflection:
>
> - Thinking back to your experiences as a student and watching your teachers teach. Was there an order in which they sequenced activities to help you learn?
> - What role did different (hands-on, minds-on) experiences play in your learning?
> - What role did explanations from teachers or textbooks have in your learning?

Our use of the term *practices* refers to the processes and strategies of teaching. Teaching practices include the unique personal dynamics between teachers and students and the various interactions among educational technologies, laboratory investigations, and myriad other teachings techniques.

An instructional sequence is as near a connection as we can get to the teaching practices unique to individuals who have a teaching style, understandings of content, set of skills, and especially knowledge of their students.

If the overarching goal of STEM instruction is for students to develop long-term understanding and the ability to transfer STEM ideas across contexts, then the way activities are structured and sequenced is an essential consideration. A well-designed sequence ensures that learning builds progressively, allowing students to connect new concepts to prior knowledge, deepen their understanding, and apply their skills in meaningful ways. Without intentional sequencing, instruction can become disjointed, leading to gaps in students' comprehension and missed opportunities for critical thinking. By carefully structuring STEM learning experiences, educators create a coherent pathway that fosters STEM literacy 21st-century workforce abilities and interest in STEM-related careers.

## Common Hands-on Science Instructional Sequences

A significant theme throughout this book is that students have a high capacity to think logically about STEM issues if they have firsthand experiences with phenomena, are encouraged to make claims based on evidence, and can develop dependable explanations. A key to learning is to create supportive classroom conditions that foster students' critical thinking about their experiences with STEM topics. Because direct experiences are so crucial in forming a more accurate understanding, they are worth further exploration when we consider practices for STEM education.

Do all instructional approaches yield the same results? Simply put, the answer is no. Not all approaches to teaching STEM intentionally build students' conceptual coherence from a cognitive standpoint (Michaels, Shouse, & Schweingruber, 2008). The influences of students' current knowledge plays a pivotal role in learning. In the early 1980s, conceptual change theory described the importance of knowledge or often referred to as "prior" knowledge or misconceptions, and the implications for learning science (Posner et al., 1982). Replacing students' current ideas i.e., misconceptions with STEM-related concepts is the process for helping students understand, test, refine, and reformulate their current conceptions based on data that they use as evidence for understanding. Misconceptions are essential to recognize from a cognitive standpoint because only if students find new ideas more compelling ideas do they change and begin to revise their initial conceptions and create new explanations about how the world works.

A strength in a well-designed sequence of instruction is the ability to promote conceptual change because ideas stimulated at the onset of instruction can be tested and investigated through learning experiences. Data and evidence based on such experiences become the basis for students' reconstructed explanations and solutions. In this view, learning activities and lesson planning require a purposeful interaction between students' current knowledge and thinking about their immediate experiences to construct accurate understanding (Bransford, Brown, & Cocking, 2000). Research on students' misconceptions supports this assertion and has shown that teaching is likely to be ineffective unless it takes learners' perspectives into account (Driver et al., 1994). It is critically important to recognize students' current at the onset of new units of study.

Common instructional sequences in classrooms can be divided into two broad categories: (1) the traditional approach, in which teachers provide explanations through before experiences; and (2) explore-before-explain, in which teachers provide experiences before explanations.

## Using a Traditional Approach to Promote STEM Learning

An example of the traditional educational sequence divides instruction into three phases: (1) inform, (2) verify, and (3) practice (Abraham, 1992). In the first phase, students are informed about what they are to learn. Lectures and textbook readings are activities to inform students about specific scientific ideas. Next, students verify knowledge introduced in lectures and readings through laboratory activities or demonstrations by which they can confirm concepts, theories, and facts with data. Finally, students answer questions or work problems to practice their new knowledge in other circumstances. Using a traditional sequence gives teachers the task of identifying major concepts and presenting them clearly and understandable to students. Once the students learn (and, in most cases, remember) new ideas, they practice them in a range of situations. Although evidence should always play a role in learning, data and students' immediate experiences are not at the heart of the traditional sequence. Instead, the teacher's explanations of ideas play an initial and central role in learning. Data support the ideas that have been constructed firsthand by students.

Although investigatory experiences can inherently be engaging for students because of their hands-on nature, for the experience to also be minds-on, these experiences must be cognitively explored, integrated with the flow of instruction, and challenge student thinking. Unfortunately, the research on laboratory experiences has revealed that too often when the experiential part of teaching is disconnected from content, students leave with a misunderstanding of the content and view content as separate from practice (Singer, Hilton, & Schweingruber, 2006). This same line of research has even shown that hands-on, when not integrated into the flow of classroom instruction, is no more effective than other instructional approaches such as e.g., lectures, discussions, or readings used in a similarly isolated fashion (Singer, Hilton, & Schweingruber, 2006). For example, merely doing a hands-on lab for activity's sake may interest students but not allow them to form an evidence-based claim. The reality is that many students come away from their K-16 experiences viewing science as primarily the collection of facts (Duschl, Schweingruber, & Shouse, 2007).

## Using an Explore-Before-Explain Approach to STEM Learning

The difference between an explore-before-explain and a traditional approach is that students have the chance to collect data and investigate [science] before being introduced to new concepts. For example, to promote learning from a learner-oriented perspective, Bransford, Brown, and Cocking (2000) suggest:

> An alternative to simply progressing through a series of exercises that derive from a scope and sequence chart is to expose students to the major patterns of a subject domain as they arise naturally in problem situations. Activities can be structured so that students are able to explore, explain, extend, and evaluate their progress. Ideas are best introduced when students see a need or a reason for their use—this helps them see relevant uses of the knowledge to make sense of what they are learning.
>
> (p. 127)

One popular contemporary approach that [promotes] explore-before-explain is the 5E (Engage, Explore, Explain, Elaborate, Evaluate) instructional model (Bybee, 1997). The phases of the 5E are closely connected to the research on cognition, acknowledging the important role of prior knowledge in learning, and the essential need to promote transfer for students.

*[Engage ➔ Explore ➔ Explain ➔ Elaborate ➔ Evaluate.]*

## The 5E Instructional Model: A Research-based Framework for Learning

The 5E Instructional Model is a widely recognized framework for designing effective science and STEM instruction, structured [around] five key phases: Engage, Explore, Explain, Elaborate, and Evaluate (Bybee, 1997, 2015). This model is grounded in constructivist learning theory, which emphasizes that learners build new knowledge by actively connecting it to prior experiences rather than passively receiving information (Bransford, Brown, & Cocking, 2000). This may seem like a simple idea, but it is not. Scholars who studied cognitive development, such as Jean Piaget, Jerome Bruner, and Lev Vygotsky, developed our primary understanding of learners and learning. The best active, learner-centered lessons [provide] experiences that deeply entrench ideas and promote long-lasting understanding. In this regard, understanding is highlighted by an individual's ability to reconstruct and apply conceptual knowledge rather than the retrieval of specific facts (NASEM, 2018). Each phase of the 5E model is designed to support how students naturally learn, moving from curiosity-driven exploration to deeper conceptual understanding and applications. Because the 5E Model aligns with how the brain processes and retains information, it serves as a powerful framework for sensemaking in STEM—helping students learn both STEM concepts and develop critical thinking, problem-solving, and communication skills that are essential for real-world applications.

## Engage: Sparking Curiosity and Creating Teachable Moments

The Engage phase of STEM instruction is designed to capture students' interest through meaningful and relevant activities. The experiences should spark curiosity, encourage questions, and motivate inquiry (Bybee, 2002). This phase not only motivates students but also elicits their current knowledge and experiences, an essential step in conceptual change—helping students refine or replace misconceptions with evidence-based understanding (Bybee, 2015).

In STEM fields, scientists and engineers begin their work by asking questions and seeking to understand phenomena or solve problems. Similarly, students should be intrigued by the learning activities during the Engage phase, mirroring the inquisitiveness of STEM professionals. Open-ended questions tied to the core content serve as catalysts for student thinking, encouraging them to ask their own questions and actively engage in the learning process.

Teachers play a crucial role in this phase by initiating and facilitating discussions that surface students' initial ideas, experiences, and preconceptions. Eliciting students' thinking at the start of an instructional sequence serves as a cognitive primer, preparing their brains for the deeper learning. The more students connect new STEM ideas with their existing knowledge, the stronger their understanding and ability to apply that knowledge in novel situations.

## Explore: Investigating STEM Concepts through Meaningful Experiences

The Explore phase immerses students in investigations that mirror the scientific and engineering practices used in STEM disciplines. During this phase, students actively engage in data collection, experimentation, and problem-solving, gathering either quantitative or qualitative data as they investigate new STEM ideas. The activities selected should be carefully designed to align with the STEM concepts being introduced.

Rather than directly explaining content, teachers guide students in investigating problems, conducting experiments, or engineering solutions through procedures that facilitate their formulations of explanations for situations under study. These experiences mirrors how scientists and engineers operate—relying on data rather than assumptions to inform their understanding. Students should focus on making observations, identifying patterns, and beginning preliminary analysis without immediate reliance on external sources.

Importantly, students should remain open to modifying their initial ideas as they analyze their findings—just as scientists revise hypotheses based on experimental data and engineers iterate their designs for proposed solutions to problems. Many exploration activities involve teamwork, fostering collaborative problem solving and modeling the way STEM professionals work in research labs and industry settings. By engaging deeply in this exploratory phase, students develop the foundational thinking skills needed for scientific discovery and technological innovation.

## Explain: Making Sense of STEM Concepts through Evidence-Based Reasoning

The Explain phase challenges students to synthesize their findings from the Engage and Explore phases and construct evidence-based explanations of

STEM concepts. At this point, students shift from investigation to making sense of phenomena using data analysis, pattern recognition, and reasoning to articulate what they have experienced. This phase mirrors the processes scientists use to develop theories based on experimental evidence and engineers use to refine their designs based on testing. Students should focus on identifying relationships, drawing conclusions, and articulating explanations grounded in their own data. Rather than looking to outside sources for validation, they use their collected evidence to justify claims, identify cause-and-effect relationships, and explain observed phenomena.

Teachers support this process by introducing scientific and engineering terminology, conceptual models, and different forms of representation, such as diagrams, equations, or analogies, to enhance students' comprehension. Providing readings or supplementary explanations at this stage is particularly powerful because students now have an initial framework to attach new vocabulary and concepts to, strengthening their ability to retain and apply their learning. The research on investigative experiences has revealed that too often when the hands-on part of learning is disconnected from content, students leave with a false understanding and view content as isolated (Singer, Hilton, & Schweingruber, 2006). This same line of research has even shown that labs, when not integrated into the flow of classroom instruction, are no more effective than other instructional approaches (e.g., lectures, discussions, or readings) used in a similarly isolated fashion (Singer, Hilton, & Schweingruber, 2006).

Additionally, teachers can introduce, or students can explore STEM career connections, highlighting how scientists, engineers, and technologists analyze data, refine their models, and communicate their findings using precise terminology and logical reasoning. By anchoring explanations in student-driven discoveries, this phase solidifies conceptual understanding and prepares students to apply their knowledge in new situations.

## Elaborate: Extending STEM Understanding Through Application and Innovation

The Elaborate phase provides students with opportunities to apply their new-found STEM knowledge to novel problems, authentic challenges, and interdisciplinary contexts. This step is crucial because STEM literacy is not just about knowing concepts—it's about the competency to apply them to solve problems and innovate.

Students engage in design challenges, engineering projects, coding tasks, or scientific investigations that require them to test and refine their ideas in new and different settings. This phase aligns with the way scientists validate theories by testing them in different conditions and engineers iterate on designs to improve functionality. Because this phase involves higher-order thinking, students may struggle with transferring their knowledge—a natural part of learning that requires explicit modeling and strategic scaffolding. Teachers support this phase by providing structured protocols, problem-solving strategies, or collaborative discussions that encourage students to transfer their ideas. By engaging in the Elaborate phase, students develop STEM habits of mind—critical thinking, creativity, and adaptability—essential skills that prepare them for the 21$^{st}$-century workforce and STEM-related careers. This phase ensures that students don't just memorize facts but can think like STEM professionals, applying knowledge to new contexts and challenges.

## Evaluate: Measuring STEM Learning and Encouraging Metacognition

The Evaluate phase is a critical component of STEM instruction, as it allows both students and teachers to assess how much learning has occurred and how well students can apply their knowledge in meaningful ways. Students reflect on how their understanding developed since the Engage phase, engaging in metacognition—an essential skill for STEM professionals, who must continuously assess their thinking and refine their approaches. Research (Hattie, 2009) suggests that metacognitive reflection significantly enhances learning, helping students recognize not just what they learned, but how they learned it. During this phase, teachers use both formative and summative assessments to determine whether students have developed conceptual knowledge and problem-solving abilities. Evaluations may take various forms, including:

- Performance tasks that require students to apply STEM concepts in new contexts,
- Engineering design challenges that assess iterative problem-solving skills,
- STEM explanations and argumentation that demonstrate reasoning and evidence-based, thinking, or
- Collaborative discussions or presentations that showcase understanding.

While this phase may include traditional assessments, it is not grading—it is about gauging STEM understanding and determining the next steps for instruction. The insights gathered can help teachers continue to identify misconceptions, adjust their future lessons, and differentiate instruction to ensure that all students build a strong STEM foundation. Ultimately, the Evaluate phase reinforces the iterative nature of STEM learning—students should see assessment as a tool for continuous improvement rather than a final endpoint.

## Conclusions

The 5E model sequence instruction so that students have ample time and opportunities with data that serve as evidence and allow them to generate deeper understandings. Students' understandings are based on their direct encounters with meaningful phenomena. The 5E instructional model has been the theme of sections in science teaching methods books (see Contant et al., 2018), and research has proven the benefits of the approach for increasing students' motivation and achievement (see Bybee et al., 2006). There is so much compelling support for learning cycle sequences that scholars have suggested the approach as a central theory of instruction (Bybee, 1997).

> **Question for Discussion:**
> 
> ♦ What would you consider as a foundation for an effective sequence of instructional practices?

## References

Abraham, M. R. (1992). Instructional strategies designed to teach science. In Lawrenz, F., Cochran, K., Krajcik, J., & Simpson, P. (Eds.), *Research Matters - to the Science Teacher* (pp. 41–50). Minneapolis, MN: NARST Monograph #5.

Bransford, J., Brown, A., & Cocking, R. (2000). *How People Learn: Brain, Mind, Experience, and School*. Washington, DC: National Academies Press.

Bybee, R. W. (1997). *Achieving Scientific Literacy: From Purposes to Practices*. Portsmouth, NH: Heinemann Educational Books.

Bybee, R. W. (Ed.) (2002). *Learning Science and the Science of Learning*. Arlington, VA: NSTA Press.

Bybee, R. W. (2015). *The BSCS 5E Instructional Model: Creating Teachable Moments*. Arlington, VA: NSTA Press.

Bybee, R. W., Taylor, J. A., Gardner, A., Van Scotter, P., Powell, J. C., Westbrook, A., & Landes, N. (2006). *The BSCS 5E Instructional Model: Origins,*

*Effectiveness, and Applications*. Colorado Springs, CO: BSCS. https://media.bscs.org/bscsmw/5es/bscs_5e_full_report.pdf

Contant, T. L., Bass, J. L., Tweed, A. A., & Carin, A. A. (2018). *Teaching Science Through Inquiry-Based Instruction* (13th ed.). New York: Pearson.

Driver, R., Squires, A., Rushworth, P., & Wood-Robinson, V. (1994). *Making Sense of Secondary Science: Research into Children's Ideas*. London: Routledge.

Duschl, R. A., Schweingruber, H. A., & Shouse, A. W. (Eds.) (2007). *Taking Science to School: Learning and Teaching Science in Grades K–8*. Washington, DC: National Academies Press.

Hattie, J. (2009). *Visible Learning: A Synthesis of Over 800 Meta-Analyses Relating to Achievement*. New York: Routledge.

Michaels, S., Shouse, A. W., & Schweingruber, H. A. (2008). *Ready, Set, Science! Putting Research to Work in K–8 Science Classrooms*. National Academies Press. https://www.nap.edu/catalog/11882/ready-set-science-putting-research-to-work-in-k-8#toc

National Academies of Sciences, Engineering, and Medicine. (2018). *How People Learn II: Learners, Contexts, and Cultures*. Washington, DC: National Academies Press.

Posner, G. J., Strike, K. A., Hewson, P. W., & Gertzog, W. A. (1982). Accommodation of a scientific conception: Toward a theory of conceptual change. *Science Education*, Vol. 66(2): pp. 211–227.

Singer, S. R., Hilton, M. L., & Schweingruber, H. A. (Eds.) (2006). *America's Lab Report: Investigations in High School Science*. Washington, DC: National Academies Press.

# Part IV
# Cultivating STEM Teacher Expertise

# 13

# Centering Efforts on the Instructional Core

This chapter lays out three essential pillars for realizing effective STEM learning. It provides a unifying framework that connects standards, curriculum, programs, and professional development. Ultimately, this chapter begins to answer the central question: How can this book equip teachers to develop robust STEM programs and effectively utilize STEM practices in their classrooms? It offers practical guidance for educators committed to implementing high-quality STEM education.

> Aim: To clarify three essential pillars necessary for making STEM learning a reality for students by exploring the connections among standards, curriculum, and professional learning.
>
> Objectives: Individuals and professional learning teams considering implementation of STEM education will:
>
> - Clarify the connection among standards, curriculum, and professional learning in STEM education.
> - Provide a practical framework of reform strategies for implementing meaningful STEM programs.

> Reflections: STEM educators will consider a number of questions:
>
> - How do you currently balance the interconnected roles of standards, curriculum, and professional learning in your approach to STEM education?
> - Where do you see the greatest challenges and successes?
> - In what ways do your leadership decisions help foster STEM literacy? Promote 21st-century workforce abilities? Enhance students' understanding and interest in STEM careers?

Leaders in STEM education are expected to act as both transformational and catalytic agents of change. They are entrusted with identifying and addressing challenges, formulating solutions based on complex problems, and responding to emerging needs within their schools, districts, and regions. These demands make the role of educational leadership inherently multifaceted and complex. Leaders must navigate a dual focus: on one hand, developing and sustaining the knowledge and skills of their teachers; on the other, ensuring that students are adequately prepared for success in K-12 STEM education and beyond.

Being a leader in STEM education also comes with significant challenges, many of which emerge from the urgency of achieving equitable and meaningful STEM literacy for all students. STEM leaders must grapple with issues of access, engagement, and relevance, striving to close persistent opportunity gaps while simultaneously raising the bar for what students can achieve. The goal is not merely to improve teaching and learning but also to transform the educational experience so that students see themselves as potentially capable of contributing to, and thriving in, STEM fields.

Achieving this vision requires leaders to balance short-term needs with long-term goals, all while navigating a rapidly evolving educational landscape. They must prioritize fostering STEM literacy in ways that go beyond simply meeting benchmarks, focusing instead on cultivating students' ability to think critically, solve complex problems, and apply interdisciplinary knowledge to real-world challenges. Leaders must also ensure that teachers are equipped with the skills, confidence, and tools to deliver high-quality STEM instruction that reflects the demands of modern standards.

In the present time and the coming decade, STEM leaders must direct their attention to the core elements of STEM education. Richard F. Elmore (2004), described the instructional core as, "By 'the core of educational practice,' I mean how teachers understand the nature of knowledge and their students' role in learning, and how these ideas about knowledge and learning are manifest in teaching and classwork" (p. 8). This quote underscores the

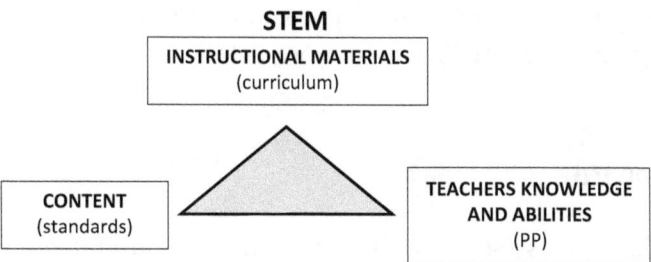

Figure 13.1 Core Elements of STEM.

critical importance of the instructional core and the interplay between teacher knowledge, instructional content, and student engagement in effective educational programs. In addition, this quote has direct implications for teacher professional learning (see Figure 13.1).

## The Role of the Instructional Core in Large-Scale Improvement

Focusing on the instructional core recognizes the complex and difficult work of STEM reform. The instructional core serves as the foundation for educational improvement, encompassing three critical elements: (1) reforming educational programs and practices in alignment with modern STEM-related standards or updated state-specific frameworks; (2) designing and implementing instructional materials, or curriculum, which translates the innovations expressed in standards into actionable learning experiences; and (3) providing robust professional learning opportunities to equip teachers with the knowledge and skills needed to effectively deliver instruction that facilitates students' learning.

These three elements—content, curriculum, and professional learning—are interdependent and can be visualized as the three legs of a stool. The stool analogy highlights the necessity of balance: just as each leg of a stool must be precisely aligned to support weight, each component of the instructional core must be thoughtfully developed and seamlessly integrated to sustain meaningful and enduring change.

## Maintaining Balance: Characteristics of Each "Leg"

Although the three-legged stool analogy may appear simplistic, it underscores the importance of precision and alignment across all components. Each "leg" contributes uniquely to the broader goal of improving learning at scale, and neglecting any one component risks undermining the entire structure. Below we explain the three "legs" in more detail.

## Modern Standards

The STEM disciplines (see Part II, "Introducing Foundation for the STEM Disciplines") and modern STEM standards provide a critical foundation for shaping instructional design and establishing clear and rigorous expectations for what students should know and be able to do at each grade level. These standards are not merely a checklist of content; they embody a vision of preparing students to navigate and thrive in a rapidly changing, technologically driven world. STEM standards are inherently forward-looking, emphasizing skills such as critical thinking, problem solving, collaborative innovation, and the application of interdisciplinary knowledge. These competencies are essential for equipping students to tackle the challenges of the 21st century, from addressing global sustainability issues to advancing technological and medical breakthroughs.

A logical place to begin is STEM standards for learning and national reform documents such as:

- Science: Next Generation Science Standards (NGSS/Lead States, 2013)
- Technology: International Society for Technology in Education (ISTE, 2000)
- Engineering: NGSS Engineering Practices (2013)
- Mathematics: Common Core State Standards (CCSS, 2010)

These national documents may be used to develop corresponding state-level Standards. What may be missing from these documents but important to consider is the integration that occurs that transcends traditional subject boundaries. For instance, students may be expected to use mathematical modeling to analyze engineering problems or apply computational thinking to scientific investigations. Using standards as a starting point helps promote a holistic understanding of STEM disciplines, reinforcing their interconnected nature and relevance to real world contexts.

When implemented effectively, modern STEM standards do more than prepare students for careers in science, technology, engineering, and mathematics; they cultivate a mindset of innovation and adaptability. These standards encourage students to think like scientists and engineers—questioning assumptions, testing hypotheses, and iterating on solutions. In doing so, they not only contribute to the development of a STEM-literate workforce but also empower students to be informed adult citizens capable of making decisions about complex societal issues.

By aligning instructional design with modern STEM standards and supporting educators through intentional leadership, schools can create dynamic learning environments where students are not only prepared for future challenges but inspired to shape the future themselves.

## Programs: Curriculum as Instruction

A standards-aligned curriculum serves as the essential bridge between the aspirational goals of modern educational standards and the practical realities of classroom teaching. The often broad and abstract language of standards must be converted into structured, and coherent learning experiences that are accessible, engaging, and academically rigorous. This translation is critical for ensuring that students not only meet benchmarks but also gain the deeper understanding and skills required to navigate real-world challenges.

At the heart of curriculum development is a commitment to evidence-based practices. Emerging research on cognition, learning science, and STEM education plays a vital role in shaping instructional materials that are designed to engage students effectively. For example, considering curricular design from a sensemaking perspective and the importance of instructional sequence, are essential to promote deeper understanding and sustained engagement.

Sensemaking and instructional sequence are components of curriculum development. A high-quality program must account for the diverse backgrounds, abilities, and experiences of students, ensuring that all learners have access to opportunities that foster success. Both sensemaking and purposeful sequence of instruction are the ability to help students transfer their learning to new and unfamiliar situations. This requires intentionally designing learning experiences that build connections across disciplines, contexts, and meaningful applications. Emerging research on learning science emphasizes the importance of coherence in the curriculum—ensuring that concepts are introduced in a logical sequence, revisited over time, and connected to broader themes and ideas.

For example, STEM programs might begin with a hands-on exploration of natural phenomena, leading students to develop foundational concepts that are later applied in engineering challenges or environmental problem-solving scenarios. Such approaches help students see the relevance of their learning and empower them to use their knowledge creatively and effectively beyond the classroom.

A well-designed program does more than align with standards; it creates a cohesive journey for students, where each lesson builds on prior knowledge and skills to deepen understanding. This orchestration of learning experiences requires careful attention to pacing, differentiation, and opportunities for reflection. It also demands the integration of varied instructional strategies to keep students actively engaged.

When aligned with standards and informed by research, a curriculum program becomes a powerful tool for transforming abstract goals into meaningful learning experiences. It not only equips students with the knowledge and skills outlined in the standards but also fosters a lifelong love of learning and a readiness to tackle complex challenges in an ever-changing world.

## Professional Learning for Standards-Based Programs

Professional learning is the cornerstone of equipping teachers with the pedagogical content knowledge and instructional strategies they need to effectively implement a standards-aligned curriculum. However, for professional learning to be impactful, it must go beyond traditional, one-off workshops or passive sessions. Instead, it should be an ongoing, collaborative, and practice-embedded process that supports teachers in continuously refining their skills and adapting to the dynamic needs of their students. The most effective professional learning is embedded in the daily work of teaching.

Educational leaders play a pivotal role in creating and sustaining a culture of continuous professional growth. Leaders must prioritize professional learning as a strategic investment, allocating time, resources, and support to ensure its success. This includes providing access to high-quality learning opportunities, fostering an environment where experimentation and reflection are valued, and recognizing and celebrating teacher growth and achievements.

Leaders must also model a commitment to lifelong learning by engaging in professional development themselves. This demonstrates to teachers the importance of growth and creates a shared culture of learning that permeates the school or district. Additionally, leaders can use data to identify areas of need, tailor professional learning to address those gaps, and measure its impact on both teaching practices and student outcomes

## Promoting Long-Lasting Change

The interconnection of three elements—modern content, instructional programs, and professional learning—requires a systemic approach to leadership.

Leaders must not only provide the vision and strategic direction but also support the structures and resources needed to ensure success. When each leg of the instructional core is intentionally designed and aligned, schools and districts are better positioned to achieve transformative improvements in student learning.

Sustained professional learning allows teachers to build expertise over time, enabling deeper understanding and integration of new instructional strategies. This includes regular opportunities to engage with content, reflect on their practice, and revisit key concepts as they gain experience. Effective professional learning frameworks often include cycles of inquiry, where teachers identify challenges in their instruction, implement targeted strategies, and analyze their impact on student outcomes. This iterative approach helps ensure that learning is not just theoretical but directly informs and improves practice.

## Conclusion

The Instructional Core framework reminds us that lasting educational reform is not achieved through isolated efforts or quick fixes. Unfortunately, underemphasizing the importance of all three instructional core elements can lead to misdirected emphasis. Instead, it requires leaders to embrace the complexity of their role, balancing the immediate needs of teachers and students with a long-term vision for systemic change focused on all three elements of the instructional core.

---

**Questions for Discussion:**

STEM educators will consider:

- ♦ In your experience, which of the following--standards, curriculum, or professional learning--is most often neglected or underdeveloped in STEM education initiatives, and what are the consequences of this imbalance?
- ♦ How can educators effectively design learning experiences that achieve these broader goals, and what are some examples of instructional strategies that promote both STEM literacy and active citizenship?

## References

Elmore, R. F. (2004). *School Reform from the Inside Out: Policy, Practice, and Performance*. Cambridge, MA: Harvard Education Press.

International Society for Technology in Education (ISTE). (2000). *National Educational Technology Standards* (NETS). Eugene, OR: Published by ISTE.

National Governors Association Center for Best Practices & Council of Chief State School Officers (NGAC and CCSSO). (2010). *Common Core State Standards*. Washington, DC: Authors.

NGSS Lead States. (2013). *Next Generation Science Standards: For States, by States*. Washington, DC: National Academies Press. www.nextgenscience.org/next-generation-sciencestandards

# 14

# Beginning with a Manageable Unit

Many educators are eager to implement STEM instruction, but may feel overwhelmed by the depth, breadth, and interdisciplinary nature of the task. This chapter provides a structured approach for a well-designed STEM unit that aligns with learning goals, instructional practices, and manageable classroom implementation. Educators often struggle with where to begin when developing STEM material. Should they begin with standards? Focus on engaging activities? Or consider assessments first? Drawing the themes of goal-setting, instructional sequencing, and assessment alignment, this chapter presents a structured process for launching a STEM unit that is both feasible and effective. Prior chapters provide a background related to the discussions of a manageable stem unit.

> Aim: To clarify the themes of Understanding by Design (UbD) and the importance of an integrated instructional sequence in an example using severe weather and climate change.
>
> Objectives: Individuals and professional learning teams considering designing STEM education will:
>
> ♦ Develop a structure for unit design that bridges STEM learning goals, with single lesson design, to the development of integrated instructional units.

Reflection: STEM educators will consider:

- How UbD can be used to develop big ideas and transfer goals.
- How lessons can be structured into coherent and purposeful, integrated instructional sequences.

## Establishing Clear Goals and Aligned Assessment

This chapter uses the Understanding by Design (UbD) framework as a robust and effective approach to constructing STEM instructional materials. *Understanding by Design* Wiggins and McTighe (2005) describes a process that will enhance STEM teachers' abilities to attain higher levels of student learning. The process is called *backward design*. Conceptually, the process is simple. Begin by identifying your desired learning outcomes, such as the performance expectations from the *NGSS*. Then determine what would count as acceptable evidence of student learning and actually design assessments that will provide evidence that students have learned competencies described in the performance expectations. Then, and only then, begin developing the activities that will provide students with opportunities to learn the concepts and practices described in the performance expectations. The primary strength of UbD lies in its emphasis on "backward design," a process that prioritizes the articulation of desired learning outcomes before planning instructional activities. This approach ensures that teaching and learning efforts are purposefully aligned with achieving significant, long-term goals.

UbD emphasized the development of students' ability to transfer their learning to novel contexts. This is particularly crucial in STEM, where the goal is not merely to memorize facts but to apply scientific and engineering principles to solve current problems. The selection of severe weather and climate change as a thematic focus for illustrating UbD's application is deliberate and strategic. These topics are not only highly relevant to contemporary societal challenges but also inherently interdisciplinary, demanding the integration of concepts and skills from various STEM domains. By grounding the curriculum in such timely complex issues, we aim to cultivate students' ability to apply STEM knowledge to address authentic problems.

## The Anatomy of the UbD Framework

By beginning with the end in mind, UbD ensures that all instructional activities are aligned with clearly defined learning goals. This clarity of purpose enhances both teacher effectiveness and student engagement. While UbD provides a structured framework, it also allows teachers the flexibility to tailor lessons and activities to meet the specific needs and resources of their students. This adaptability is essential in STEM education, where diverse learning styles and access to resources significantly impacts instruction.

Table 14.1 provides Stage 1 of a UbD template that illustrates the connections between Big Ideas, Transfer Goals, and Standards. This is one perspective on how teachers and curriculum specialists can tackle STEM unit design for teaching about climate change and severe weather connected to standards.

We chose to focus on middle and high school level standards to illustrate the discussion. It is important the competencies students should develop as a result of classroom practices. UbD promotes a shift from superficial coverage of content to the development of deep understanding. By focusing on big ideas and essential questions, teachers encourage students to think critically and make meaningful connections among concepts. We should also note that the Big Ideas and Transfer Goals are specific actions for assessments but not lessons, instructional units, actual tests, or other forms of assessments. UbD promotes the use of relevant problems, and scenarios.

This helps students to see the value of STEM in their daily lives.

The Big Ideas and Transfer Goals embody key ideas in each STEM discipline. The relationship between the Big Ideas and Transfer goals is evidence by the roles of standards.

Each standard's connection is tied to essential questions that students can explore through individual lessons that combine into a coherent instructional unit. We can further dissect the standards and essential questions to the knowledge and skill acquisitions desired of the STEM lessons and the unit as a whole.

Stage 1 of the UbD design process ensures that your STEM unit addresses core content, i.e., learning outcomes. Stage 1 helps you define what evidence of student learning will look like:

- Connects scientific concepts (e.g., energy transfer, atmospheric dynamics) to actual phenomena (e.g., hurricanes, heatwaves).
- Promotes critical thinking about the causes and consequences of climate change.
- Empowers students to develop and evaluate potential solutions to mitigate the impacts of severe weather.
- Builds data analysis skills through the use of weather data.
- Encourages students to communicate scientific findings effectively.

In the context of this example, consider performance tasks to measure real-world application. By adhering to these criteria, you can ensure that the

**TABLE 14.1** Stage 1 of the UbD Unit STEM Template

## Stage 1 Desired Results

| Big Ideas | Transfer |
|---|---|
| **Design Consideration 1: Clarity in Goals and Learning Outcomes for STEM Severe Weather and Climate Change Unit** ||
| • Human activities such as burning fossil fuels influence the Earth's climate and contribute to extreme weather events.<br>• Advancements in technology and engineering help scientists track, predict, and mitigate the effects of severe weather.<br>• Mathematical models allow scientists to analyze climate date and predict future weather | *Students will be able to independently use their learning to…*<br><br>• Analyze real-time weather data to make predictions about upcoming storm systems.<br>• Evaluate how different climate policies impact severe weather trends.<br>• Use engineering design principles to develop solutions for reducing the impact of climate change. |
| **Meaning** ||
| Understandings | Essential Questions |
| *Students will understand that…* | *Students will keep considering…* |
| • **Science:** The release of greenhouse gases contributes to climate change, leading to more frequent and intense weather events (NGSS, 2013).<br>• **Technology:** Advanced radar and satellite technology allow meteorologists to track storms and improve disaster preparedness (ISTE, 2000).<br>• **Engineering:** Engineers develop solutions to mitigate severe weather impacts, such as flood barriers and heat-resistant building materials (NGSS, 2013).<br>• **Mathematics:** Climate models use statistical analysis and data trends to predict future weather patterns (CCSS, 2010). | • **Science:** How does climate change influence the frequency and intensity of severe weather events?<br>• **Technology:** How do technological advancements improve our ability to predict and respond to severe weather?<br>• **Engineering:** What role do engineers play in designing infrastructure that can withstand extreme weather?<br>• **Mathematics:** How do scientists use mathematical models to predict future climate trends? |

## Stage 1 Desired Results

| Big Ideas | Transfer | |
|---|---|---|
| **Design Consideration 1: Clarity in Goals and Learning Outcomes for STEM Severe Weather and Climate Change Unit** | | |
| ◆ Climate data a predict future weather patterns. | **Acquisition** | |
| | *Students will learn about…* | *Students will be skilled at…* |
| | <ul><li>Science: Greenhouse gases and explain their role in the Earth's climate system.</li><li>Technology: Identify types of meteorological technology (e.g., Doppler radar, weather satellites, computer models).</li><li>Engineering: Identify and describe engineering solutions designed to reduce severe weather impacts (e.g., seawalls, green infrastructure, permeable pavement).</li><li>Mathematics: Analyze historical climate data using basic statistical measures (mean, median, mode, variability).</li></ul> | <ul><li>Using patterns and causal relationships to identify trends in data that serve as evidence for STEM claims.</li><li>Conduct investigations that produce data.</li><li>Communicate understandings using data that serves as evidence.</li></ul> |

STEM curricula are both rigorous and relevant, preparing students to become informed and engaged citizens in an increasingly complex world.

## Promoting Learning Essential Elements and Impactful Instructional Sequences

This section emphasizes the practical application of the Understanding by Design (UbD) framework to develop lessons that actively engage students' learning. Learning in this context refers to the process by which students construct understanding of phenomena through inquiry, exploration, and reflection. UbD's "backward design" approach is crucial for aligning instruction with desired learning out comes, ensuring that every lesson contributes to the overarching goals of the unit, which, in our example, are related to understanding severe weather and climate change.

By starting with the end in mind, defining Big Ideas and Transfer Goals, teachers can design lessons that are purposeful and relevant, fostering deeper understanding rather than superficial memorization. The lessons prioritize student engagement in active learning, where students are not passive recipients of information but active constructors of knowledge. These lessons encourage students to explore phenomena, ask questions, collect and analyze data, and develop their own explanations. The emphasis is on students "making sense" of the world around them, rather than simply memorizing facts.

We define "lessons" as focused learning experiences that helps students develop understanding of a specific topic, representing the basic building block of a curriculum, providing students with opportunities to engage in meaningful learning activities. While individual lessons are important, they should be part of a coherent sequence of activities that build upon each other, aligning with UbD's emphasis on long-term learning and transfer. By connecting lessons to a larger unit, teachers can help students see the interconnectedness of concepts and develop a deeper understanding of the subject.

The topic of severe weather and climate change provides a rich context for learning because it is relevant to students' lives, interdisciplinary, complex, and authentic. By exploring this topic, students can develop a deeper understanding of STEM concepts and their real-world applications. Therefore, lessons should begin with a phenomenon or problem that sparks student curiosity, students should have opportunities to collect and analyze data lessons should incorporate opportunities for students to reflect on their learning, teachers should facilitate students' clarification of content and lessons should be designed to build upon each other, creating a coherent learning progression.

In essence, this section advocates for shift from traditional, teacher-centered instruction to student-centered, inquiry-based learning. By using UbD, teachers can create engaging and effective STEM lessons that help students develop a deep understanding of severe weather and climate change, and, more importantly, the ability to apply that understanding to new and relevant situations.

## The Anatomy of a Lesson Sequence for Severe Weather and Climate Change

The challenge in moving from the UbD framework to a meaningful lesson is pinpointing topic and skills students must begin to develop to be prepared to address the overarching transfer goals. Coherent learning experiences are key to these lessons.

To illustrate the learning process, let's target the key understanding that students should develop related to severe weather and how climate change relates to energy transfer. Energy transfer, highlighted in the NGSS science standards, is crucial for understanding atmospheric and oceanic heat movement and its impact on weather. Students' experiences with heat transfer provide a foundation for this exploration.

The lesson should begin with a relevant phenomenon that sparks curiosity, elicits student ideas, and aligns with meaningful applications. For instance, the common sayings "close the refrigerator door or you'll let the cold out" and "close the front door, you're letting the heat out" can initiate a discussion about heat transfers. This leads to understanding how heat transfers from the Earth's surface to the atmosphere, fueling severe weather conditions and relating to climate change.

Students can test their ideas about heat transfer through simple explorations. Using an Erlenmeyer flask, beakers, hot and cold water, and food coloring, they can create a scientific model to explain and test predictions about thermal energy transfer (Note: a video resource is here: https://www.youtube.com/watch?v=xLA1EiXUCuM). This hands-on activity allows students to make evidence-based claims about the direction of heat transfer.

Enhancing understanding through explanations and further explorations is a critical component. Here, STEM explanations like "convection" can be introduced. Students can further test the effects of varying temperatures and design setups to mitigate heat transfer. They can also use weather maps to predict severe storms based on temperature differences. Finally, students should reflect on their learning journey, revisiting their initial ideas in light of data to construct more STEM-accurate explanations. This reflection process develops STEM knowledge and skills, enabling students to tackle future problems.

This 2- to 3-day sequence of lessons, using the explore-before-explain structure, emphasizes the importance of students doing the intellectual work to prepare them for other challenges (see Table 14.2).

## 5E Instructional Sequence

Expanding conceptions from single lessons to an integrated instructional sequence is essential when using the Understanding by Design (UbD) framework for practical classroom instruction. Individual lessons, while valuable, often lack the sustained engagement necessary for students to fully grasp complex STEM concepts. Integrated instructional units, however, provide the necessary time and opportunities for students to solidify their developing understanding, moving beyond isolated activities to a more coherent learning experience. The 5E Instructional Model and the *NGSS* provide practical ways to apply the backward design process. Say you identified a unit and performance expectations for severe weather and climate change. One would review concepts and practices to determine the acceptable evidence of learning. For instance, students would need to use evidence to construct an explanation clarifying severe weather and describe the patterns of climate change. Using the 5E Instructional Model, one could first design an evaluate activity – for example, and design a rubric with the aforementioned criteria. Then, one would proceed to design the *engage, explore, explain, and elaborate* experiences. As necessary, the process would be iterative between the *evaluate* phase and other activities as the development process progresses. Figure 14.1 presents the backward design process and the 5E Instructional Model.

Integrated units maintain the essential features of learning, embedding them throughout applicable lesson activities. This ensures students are actively involved in constructing their knowledge rather than passively receiving information. A crucial component of these sequences is the provision of multiple experiences with data that serve as evidence for developing understanding. Students engage in activities that require them to analyze, interpret, and utilize data to support their claims, fostering critical thinking and scientific reasoning skills. Furthermore, a key feature of an integrated sequence is the deliberate linking and integration of students' evidence-based

**TABLE 14.2** Lesson Examples Connected to STEM Disciplines for Severe Weather and Climate Change

| Lesson Component | Description | STEM Discipline Connection | Example |
|---|---|---|---|
| Phenomenon Introduction | Present a real-world scenario or problem that sparks student curiosity and relates to the targeted learning objectives. | Science (Earth Science, Physics) | Discussing why storms strengthen as ocean water temperature increases to learn about thermal energy transfer, linking the event to natural phenomena. |
| Initial Idea Elicitation | Encourage students to share their existing ideas and experiences related to the phenomenon, identifying prior knowledge and misconceptions. | Science (Physics), Engineering (Design thinking, brainstorming) | Students discussing their understanding of why their houses get hot or cold and ideas around heat or cold "escaping" when doors are open. |
| Hands-on Exploration | Students engage in hands-on activities, collecting data, and observing patterns to test their ideas and develop a deeper understanding of the concepts. | Science (Physics, Chemistry), Engineering (Experimentation) | Using Erlenmeyer flasks and beakers to observe and record the movement of dyed water in varying temperature setups, and creating a model that visualizes the path of energy transfer. |
| Explanations and Expansion | Students use evidence from their explorations to construct explanations, connect to scientific concepts, and explore further applications. | Science (Earth Science, Physics), Technology (Data analysis, modeling), Engineering (Material testing) | Discussing convection currents in relation to storm formation, analyzing weather maps to predict storm severity, and designing insulation materials. |
| Reflection and Metacognition | Students reflect on their learning journey, comparing initial ideas to final understandings and identifying areas of growth and learning | All STEM Disciplines | Students compare their pre-experiment sketches of what happens with heat transfer, to the final model or conclusions, explaining the changes and reasons why, connecting it to climate |
| Mathematical Analysis | Apply mathematical principles to explain and predict real world phenomena | Mathematics, Science | Students use temperature data and formulas to analyze heat transfer rates and to predict changes in storm intensity. |

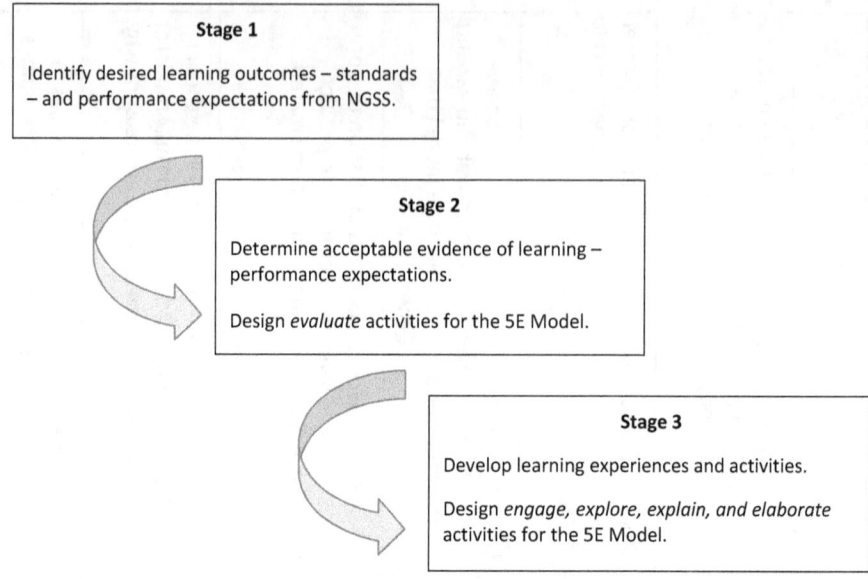

Figure 14.1 Backward Design Process and the 5E Instructional Model.

| Engage Lesson(s) | → | Exploratory Lesson(s) | → | Explanation Lesson(s) | → | Elaboration Lesson(s) | → | Evaluation Lesson(s) |

Figure 14.2 Integrated Instructional Sequence.

experiences with other learning activities within the unit. This interconnectedness ensures that learning is not compartmentalized but rather builds upon itself, creating a cohesive and meaningful learning progression. By connecting data analysis with modeling, problem-solving, and their activities, students gain a deeper understanding of how different concepts and skills relate to each other, enhancing their ability to transfer their knowledge to new contexts.

We advocate the 5E instructional sequence (Engage, Explore, Explain, Elaborate, and Evaluate), to connect students' STEM hands-on experiences with other types of learning that include reading, discussions, and lectures (see Figure 14.2).

## The Anatomy of a 5E Instructional Sequence: Connecting Sever Weather and Climate Change to STEM Disciplines

An integrated instructional sequence like the 5E allows curriculum designers and teachers the flexibility to develop lessons according to their unique teaching context and resources. While choosing individual lesson activities is up to the lesson designer, the 5E sequence should be retained due to the deeper purposes for learners and learning (Bybee, 2020).

Following the severe weather and climate change example, an integrated 5E instructional unit would start with an engagement phase activity. The purpose of the *engagement* phase is to elicit students' ideas and experiences and motivate learning. Students might consider specific severe weather instances in their lives. For example, extreme heat has been experienced by students around the world. They may consider their personal experiences, newspaper reports, and historical temperature trends. Students should provide STEM-related reasons for their thinking about why severe weather exists and whether recent trends are similar to or different from normal weather patterns.

The *exploration* phase affords students opportunities with data that serve as evidence for their understanding. Here is where the lesson on thermal energy transfer would fit into an integrated 5E instructional sequence. The lesson allows students to construct claims that thermal energy only transfers in one direction, from hot to cold. The thermal energy lesson pairs well with students using weather maps to explain and predict instances that might bring about severe weather. Students might also explore the heating and transfer of energy that occurs through different materials.

Next, students should have chances to explain their developing understandings, and teachers can introduce ideas not easily accessible from firsthand experience. The beginning of the *explanation* phase offers students the chance to articulate their evidence-based claims. Depending on the grade span, teachers might introduce how different molecules in the atmosphere and changes to these particles over time influence Earth's heating and energy transfer. They might have students discuss human growth trends and resource use over time and their influences on Earth. The goal in the explain phase is for students to deepen their understandings and use STEM-related vocabulary.

The *elaboration* phase provides students with a chance to reflect on their learning. They have chances to think about how their ideas developed over time and the factors that facilitated or constrained their understandings. For teachers, evaluation phase activities provide a means of assessing student understanding. In the context of the severe weather example, students might write an argumentative paper detailing a proposed solution to lesson severe weather drawing on learnings from the engage through elaboration phases. They may offer a prototype or build a structure that can lessen heat transfer in urban regions (for example, lessen heat island impacts). They may give a presentation about factors they determine change, then the lasting impacts could lessen severe weather and climate change. Table 14.3 summarizes a 5E integrated instructional sequence for teaching about severe weather and climate change.

**TABLE 14.3** Integrating STEM Disciplines within a 5E Instructional Sequence

| 5E Phase | Description | STEM Disciplinary Connections | Example |
|---|---|---|---|
| Engagement | Elicit student ideas and experiences, motivate learning, and connect to real-world context. | Science (Earth Science, Environmental Science), Technology (Data analysis, information literacy) | Students sharing personal experiences with severe weather events (heatwaves, storms (analyzing news reports, and exploring historical temperature trends, asking what causes these changes. |
| Exploration | Students engage in hands-on activities, collect data, and test initial ideas, like the thermal energy transfer lesson. | Science (Physics, Chemistry), Engineering (Experimentation, data collection), Mathematics (Data measuring, graphing) | Conducting experiments with Erlenmeyer flasks and beakers to observe heat transfer, using weather maps to predict severe weather conditions based on temperature differences, testing which materials retain heat. |
| Explanation | Students articulate evidence-based claims, refine understandings with STEM terminology, and make connections to scientific concepts. | Science (Physics, Earth Science, Chemistry), Technology (Scientific visualization, modeling) | Explaining convection currents using molecular models, defining terms like "thermal energy" and "convection," and describing how atmospheric changes affect heat transfer, modeling greenhouse effect and changes to it. |
| Elaboration | Students apply learned concepts to new situations, solve problems, and extend their understanding. | Science (Physics Materials Science), Engineering (Design, prototyping), Mathematics (applied math calculations) | Designing and building insulation systems to mitigate heat transfer creating urban planning solutions to reduce heat island effects, calculating effects of increased surface temperatures on water evaporation and thus humidity. |
| Evaluation | Students reflect on their learning journey, assess their understanding, and communicate their findings. | All STEM Disciplines (scientific writing, presentation), Engineering (design report, presentation) | Writing argumentative papers proposing solutions to lessen severe weather, prototyping heat-reducing structures, creating presentations about climate change mitigation strategies, building a mathematical model to represent changes in heat transfer over a specific period. |

## Conclusion

Drawing upon the principles of Understanding by Design and emphasizing the significance of a cohesive instructional sequence, this chapter has outlined a structured approach for developing a manageable STEM unit. By focusing on clear learning goals and their alignment with instructional practices and assessments, educators can confidently embark on STEM integration. The example of severe weather and climate change illustrates how big ideas and transfer goals can be translated into coherent lessons that build upon one another into integrated 5E instructional sequences. Ultimately, this framework empowers educators to move beyond feeling overwhelmed and to effectively design and implement engaging and impactful STEM learning experiences for their students.

---

**Questions for Discussion:**

STEM educators will consider:

- How can the Understanding by Design (UbD) framework be adapted to address the specific challenges of integrating multiple STEM disciplines in a cohesive unit?
- In what ways can the 5E Instructional Model be utilized to promote deeper student engagement and understanding in a STEM unit focused on complex real-world issues like severe weather and climate change?
- How can educators effectively balance the need for structured instructional sequences with the flexibility to address diverse student needs and incorporate emerging technologies in a STEM classroom?

---

## References

Bybee, R. W. (2020). *STEM, Standards, and Strategies for High-Quality Units*. Arlington, VA: NSTA Press.

Wiggins, G. P., & McTighe, J. (2005). *Understanding by Design*. Alexandria, VA: Association for Supervision and Curriculum Development.

# 15

# Enhancing Learning

## Essential Practices and Impactful Instructional Sequences

This chapter provides a structured approach for a well-designed STEM unit that aligns with learning goals, instructional practices, and manageable classroom implementation. While the previous chapter on "Beginning with a Manageable Unit," provides teachers guidance for putting programs and policies into practice, the innovations required for curriculum development should be further grounded in how students learn STEM best. This chapter includes five practical considerations for using STEM practices to help students make sense of their world. Recommendations in the chapter synthesize contemporary learning theory and classroom instruction.

> Aim: To clarify the theme of learning and the connections to STEM practices.
>
> Objectives: Individuals and professional learning teams considering implementation of STEM education will:
>
> - Make connections between learning and STEM practices,
> - Bridge the theory of learning and instructional sequences and teaching practices.
>
> Reflection Questions: STEM educators will consider:
>
> - Their experiences as a student watching teachers teach. Was there an order in which teachers sequenced activities to help you learn?

> ♦ What role did hands-on, minds-on experiences play in your learning?
> ♦ What role did explanations from teachers or textbooks have in your learning?

When engineers build a bridge, they choose durable materials that one assumes will last many decades. Just as an engineer makes designs, plans, and constructs a bridge to connect two points, a teacher builds a pathway of knowledge and skills that connects students to new understandings and opportunities. The stability and strength of the bridge depends on the quality of the engineering, just as students' learning and growth rely on the effectiveness of the learning experiences. In any construction project, you might need to slow down, refurbish specific components, and renovate in order to modernize. Implementing teaching practices in classrooms may take some time, but it is well worth the payoff.

Our approach to promoting learning is analogous to building a bridge. We propose a fundamental *if-then* proposition for STEM learning. Suppose the primary goal of modern education is to equip students with the ability to think critically and solve problems that exist in their lives so they can transfer their learning to new situations. In that case, teachers should revise existing curriculum programs and lessons, along with developing learning experiences to help students make sense of STEM concepts and allow for authentic transfer rather than creating long lists of discrete topics or skills to cover. The desired STEM understandings from firsthand experience can provide the foundation for building student knowledge.

Promoting teaching practices is key in contemporary thoughts about how to make learning more impactful and equip students with the skills and knowledge to be more self-sufficient learners. Learning experiences require students to actively figure out how the world works (science) or how to design solutions to problems (engineering) for example. A useful framework for promoting learning includes the convergence of three independent ideas: (1) the focus of modern education on teaching for understanding and transfer; (2) the application of contemporary learning theory; and (3) a purposeful sequence of instruction with those ends in mind. In its essence, the three ideas will help educators identify the big ideas that they want students to understand at a deep level in order to transfer their learning to new situations.

There are two primary reasons why focusing on teaching practices is needed at this time. One is that there are new understandings of teaching and learning that have developed over time. We see the root basis for this position in comprehensive reviews of research literature such as *How People Learn* (Bransford et al., 2000), and *How People Learn II: Learners, Contexts, and Cultures* (National Academies of Sciences, Engineering, and Medicine (NASEM), 2018). Effecting teaching rests on a single premise with far-reaching implications: If we want to promote more powerful learning for students, we need to ground our instructional practices in modern research on how students learn. The second is the opportunity to better prepare students for the reality of their world through more meaningful classroom experiences. Here we describe essential planning considerations tied to research and ways to sequence these essential elements to maximize learning.

## Consideration 1: Activating Student Ideas

As STEM educators, we have an extraordinary opportunity to activate learning.

Activating learning is hallmarked by two key features: engaging students' prior ideas and motivating further development of knowledge through questions or problems relevant to students' lives. Using "natural integrators" (e.g., place-based cases, questions, project/problem-based scenarios)—does precisely what is called for in effective lessons. The term "natural" is used to situate learning in instances that are meaningful and relevant to students because they exist in their personal experiences. "Integrators" refers to the opportunities to make connections between new and students' current existing ideas (i.e., misconceptions).

Research strongly supports these assertions about the importance of activating student thinking and explanation. Students come to school as knowledge even before being taught anything. They have lived for some years and constructed ideas about how the world works from everyday interactions with their environment, family, friends, and media. In short, they have made sense of their world. Students have become knowers through their firsthand experiences which provide evidence for their ideas. Our students do not enter school as empty vessels waiting to be filled with knowledge. Instead, they arrive with unique ideas about phenomena and mental practices underpinning some of the ways to generate more reliable and valid understanding. Although most of us would not label students' innate ways of knowing their world with terms like "content," "practices," and "ways to generate reliable and valid understanding," studies on the cognition of early learning show that kids' play is an attempt to explore things, similar to the way scientists learn things through experimentation (Gopnik, Meltzoff, & Kuhl, 1999). Even young children learn about the likelihood of something happening based on another event occurring. The idea that young children think in ways similar to scientists is not something students develop out of intellectually. Characteristics of learners and learning are similar throughout our lifespan and emphasize the important role that prior knowledge plays in constructing new ideas (Bransford, Brown & Cocking, 2000). We can tap into intuitive explorations, problem solving, and inquiry skills that students bring to school. Leveraging students' current knowledge and skills can be a powerful launching pad for deeper understanding.

Beginning lessons with students' current ideas and experiences and transitioning to new experiences ripe for exploration creates a "need-to-know" situation that engages their learning. A well-chosen STEM topic will be something that students experience in their lives and invoke curiosity and questions about their experiences. Research studies show that targeting regional or global phenomena related to citizens to help make learning relevant to students. In addition, using global or regional concerns, problems/projects (Krajcik & Czerniak, 2018), place-based scenarios (Gruenewald, 2003), or socio-scientific issues (Zeidler & Kahn, 2014) that are grade-span-appropriate are research-based ways to situate learning. Regardless of the approach used to motivate learning, students should experience phenomena or problems together and share their observations and questions to create a community of learners.

A key feature of exploratory lessons is that they engage all students, not just those that may have previously been labeled as already "STEM-minded." On a basic level, "notice" and "wonder" talk routines around natural integrators can provide practical discourse frameworks to help move to more equitable learning experiences about scientific occurrences for all students.

Asking "What do you notice?" about a STEM-related situation invites uninhibited participation (i.e., not tied to fears of assessing ideas) and elicits students' insights based on their experiences. Said differently, asking what you notice invites the voices of students who may often be silent in the classroom. Questions like "What do you wonder?" are among the highest-yield instructional practices since they focus students' attention and create a need to know (McTighe & Willis, 2019). Using notice and wonderment questions reveals students' exploration and experiences and can lead to evidence gathering. Once wonderment questions are identified, students can predict their ideas based on rules from their prior knowledge and experiences. When students think about an event, and their experiences, and provide reasons for their thinking, they engage in making sense of their world. Using students' ideas and experiences about content at the beginning of lessons bridges learning experiences so students can make sense of new ideas.

Anchoring lessons in students' prior experiences and their wonderment focuses learning on pursuing answers to questions or solutions to problems that students share.

## Consideration 2: Constructing Evidence-Based Claims

Focusing on evidence-based claims is a powerful way to teach in a STEM-standards-minded manner. Students can only arrive at an evidence-based claim through the unique combination of disciplinary core ideas, science and engineering practices, and crosscutting concepts—all foundational elements of modern science education standards. By nesting the appropriate Science and Engineering Practices and Crosscutting Concepts within the lesson, STEM teachers can ensure that students develop a deep understanding of the underlying concepts using practices and logical thinking. This is crucial if we want students to use STEM fields, particularly science, to understand and explain their world.

Focusing on evidence-based claims in STEM education not only aligns with but also can help operationalize the goals of performance expectations (PEs) from the NGSS, ensuring that students engage in authentic STEM practices that deepen their understanding and prepare them for real-world problem-solving. While not all PEs explicitly require students to make evidence-based claims as the central focus, this skill remains a foundational aspect of STEM education. For instance, when evaluating models, testing designs, or describing phenomena—core activities in STEM—students often need to justify their conclusions or choices based on observations, making the practice of evidence-based reasoning valuable across STEM disciplines. Said a bit differently and to illustrate with a specific example, while many PEs focus on students developing or using models, the importance of evidence-based claims is essential for the assertions students construct from model-based thinking, indirectly involved in justifying their model choices and communicating their STEM findings. Thus, pinpointing the evidence-based claims students can make and applying them to more specific PEs can help STEM teachers bridge the frameworks to practice.

## Consideration 3: Enhancing STEM Understandings

Students often need enhancement activities to help them explain meanings they have made and transfer their learning to new situations. Enhancements confront limits in current understanding and establish where to go next in learning. Deciding on enhancements that build on students developing knowledge requires clarity about the STEM content, practices, and critical and logical thinking skills desired from classroom experiences. There is too much content to cover it all in a school year. Enhancement activities should focus on essential questions that need answering for sophisticated STEM understanding.

Teachers can plan for the essential vocabulary and terms for concepts and processes related to students' firsthand experiences that fill gaps from the explorations and are necessary for a successful understanding of STEM. In addition, explanations allow students to have shared ways to communicate specialized STEM terminologies that represent bigger, more overarching, conceptual ideas. Readings, discussions, and lectures become rich learning experiences because they connect ideas and students' frameworks for understanding and addressing essential questions. STEM-related standards are good places to begin when identifying essential academic vocabulary for and developing classroom discussions.

Teachers can also plan for further explorations that allow students to use terms and concepts in new and different investigations to promote transfer learning (McTighe & Willis, 2019). Elaborations in the form of further topics and experiences let students test the utility of content, practices, and logical thinking to see how well their abilities generalize to answer new questions and solve different problems.

## Consideration 4: Reflecting on Developing Understanding

Planning lessons and units should offer students opportunities to think about what they have learned and how far they have come intellectually—engaging in *metacognition*, which significantly affects learning (Bransford, Brown, & Cocking, 2000). Evaluation from a learner's perspective is tied to their current knowledge and a chance to assess how ideas have developed and strategies that lead to more reliable and valid evidence-based claims. Students should have opportunities to accurately self-assess; they should be able to reflect on their learning; they should set future learning goals. Students should continually reflect on where they have been and where they are going. Studies show that students who engage in ideas inherent in their own questions and develop strong metacognitive skills and are positioned to learn more and perform better than peers who are still developing their abilities to reflect on understanding (Wang et al., 1990). Finally, John Hattie's (2023) landmark meta-analyses of more than 800 research studies ranked self-reported grades, now termed "student visible learning" (i.e., students thinking about their understanding), as the second most influential factor influencing student achievement.

## Consideration 5: Sequence of Instruction

Now, we need to consider how helping students make sense of life situations related to STEM can be developed in ways that promote critical thinking and problem solving. For example, the strategies used to engage students' ideas should come first in the instructional sequence. The engagement strategies activate student thinking by eliciting prior ideas and experiences and make learning relevant when connected to occurrences in their lives. Next, students should have exploration opportunities to construct claims based on evidence. Then, teachers can use enhancements to introduce ideas that are not easily assessable firsthand and STEM-related terms and concepts that summarize conceptual ideas or sophisticated understanding. Finally, students should have opportunities to think about their learning and reflect on what works to develop a more accurate understanding. The critical point is that once the essential features of learning are considered, they can be arranged into an instructional sequence to engage students and promote long-lasting conceptual understanding.

## Conclusion

In closing, successful planning may be easier to accomplish by not having a linear expectation for completing the work. But it is essential to make the case for a few design features, to be clear, while we begin our instruction with students' current ideas, our planning benefits from first identifying the evidence-based claims students can make from experiences. Constructing an evidence-based claim forces students to do the hard intellectual work. Students' evidence-based claims are key outcomes in learning. Other essential elements can emerge from the evidence-based claims teachers use to orchestrate STEM learning for students. When evidence-based claims are identified first in our planning, teachers can work backwards to decide phenomena or problems to activate student thinking and elicit their ideas. In addition, through students' exploratory experiences teachers and students can decide where to go next in learning. Finally, throughout the process, students should think about where they have been and are going as learners as well as the strategies and activities that help them develop more STEM-minded understandings. If we do these things in our practices, we can expect more than incremental changes by zeroing in on high-leverage instructional practices. We can expect to see what Michael Fullan (2010) calls "stunningly powerful consequences" for students.

> **Questions for Discussion:**
>
> STEM educators will consider:
>
> - How can STEM educators effectively integrate "natural integrators" like place-based scenarios or socio-scientific issues into their teaching to activate students' prior knowledge and create a "need-to-know" situation that motivates learning?
> - The document emphasizes the importance of students constructing evidence-based claims. How can educators design learning experiences that support students in developing these claims, and what strategies can be used to help students connect their claims to broader STEM principles?
> - Reflecting on learning and metacognition are presented as essential components of effective STEM education. What are some practical ways educators can incorporate opportunities for students to reflect on their developing understanding, assess their learning strategies, and set future learning goals within the context of a STEM unit or lesson?

## References

Bransford, J. D., Brown, A. L., & Cocking, R. R. (2000). *How People Learn: Brain, Mind, Experience, and School.* Washington, DC: National Academies Press.

Fullan, M. (2010). *Motion Leadership: The Skinny on Becoming Change Savvy.* Thousand Oaks, CA: Corwin.

Gopnik, A., Meltzoff, A. N., & Kuhl, P. K. (1999). *The Scientist in the Crib: Minds, Brains, and How Children Learn.* New York: William Morrow & Co.

Gruenewald, D. A. (2003). *The Best of Both Worlds: A Critical Pedagogy of Place. Educational Researcher* (Vol. 32: pp. 3–12). Thousand Oaks, CA: Sage Publishing.

Hattie, J. (2023). *Visible Learning: The Sequel: A Synthesis of Over 2,100 Meta-Analyses Relating to Achievement* (1st ed.). New York and London: Routledge. https://doi.org/10.4324/9781003380542

Krajcik, J. S., & Czerniak, C. M. (2018). *Teaching Science in Elementary and Middle School: A Project-Based Learning Approach* (5th ed.). New York and London: Routledge, Taylor & Francis Group.

McTighe, J., & Willis, J. (2019). *Upgrade Your Teaching: Understanding by Design Meets Neuroscience.* Alexandria, VA: ASCD.

Wang, M. C., Haertel, G. D., & Walberg, H. J. (1990). What influences learning? A content analysis of review literature. *Journal of Educational Research*, Vol. 84(1): pp. 30–43.

Zeidler, D. L., & Kahn, S. (2014). *It's Debatable!: Using Socioscientific Issues to Develop Scientific Literacy, K-12*. Arlington, VA: National Science Teachers Association Press.

# Part V
# Developing District-Wide STEM Programs and Practices

# 16

# Establishing a Plan for Change

The increasing availability of STEM curriculum resources necessitates a thoughtful and systematic approach to evaluation. This chapter addresses the critical need for a systematic evaluation of the increasing number of available STEM curriculum resources. The chapter aims to provide STEM educators with a structured approach to evaluate these resources and materials, ensuring they align with effective STEM education principles. It discusses the decisions schools and districts face when choosing instructional STEM materials, including whether to purchase from commercial publishers, utilize open education resources, or explore other online options. The chapter emphasizes the importance of a thoughtful and informed decision-making process, driven by the goal of enhancing student learning through effective resource utilization.

---

Aims: To provide STEM educators with a structured approach for evaluating curriculum resources and materials to ensure alignment with effective STEM education principles.

Objectives: Individuals and professional learning teams involved in selecting or developing STEM materials will:

- Individuals and professional learning teams involved in selecting or developing STEM materials will be able to apply a structured approach to evaluate curriculum resources for alignment with effective STEM education principles.
- Individuals and professional learning teams will be able to identify key factors to prioritize when choosing STEM instructional materials from various sources (commercial, open education, online) to ensure they effectively support student learning.

Reflections: STEM educators will consider:

- Given the various options for acquiring STEM instructional materials (commercial publishers, open education resources, online sites), what factors should be prioritized in the selection process to ensure the chosen materials effectively support student learning and align with STEM education principles in your specific context?
- How can a preliminary cost–risk–benefit review, as described in the chapter, help schools and districts make informed decisions about adopting STEM materials, and what are the potential trade-offs that educators should be prepared to address in this process?

## Selecting Instructional Resources for STEM

Consider this: Your school (or district) has decided to implement instructional STEM materials. As a leader, you realize the need for instructional STEM units and must make a choice. Should the school (or district) purchase available instructional materials from commercial publishers, open education resources, or other online sites? Too often, this decision is made with only cursory consideration. The initial questions regarding the decision-making process vary but go something like this: "My district has decided to adopt a standards-aligned program; which is the best available?," "Because of budget restrictions, we must find and purchase materials that align with the standards; what is the best way to proceed?" Regardless of the decision made by leadership regarding new instructional materials, it's important to acknowledge that teachers are fundamentally driven by the desire for the best possible outcome: the effective use of resources to enhance student learning. Furthermore, professional development should be an integral part of the selection, adaptation, or development process, no matter which path is chosen.

## Evaluating the Decision: A Preliminary Approach

To make an informed initial decision, leaders should conduct a preliminary, qualitative cost–risk–benefit review of the three options. This review could include asking:

- **Cost**: What are the costs of each proposed solution? What are the school's (or district's) exact needs? Can state support offset any costs? What is the total cost, including any "hidden" costs (e.g., material replacement, new STEM equipment)? Are current facilities and equipment adequate for the new units? What is the professional development cost for each option? These are initial questions; others will emerge.
- **Risk**: What are the risks related to consumable replenishment, professional learning, and alignment with standards and assessments?
- **Benefit**: How will the materials benefit teachers and student learning? Is there evidence for alignment of standards? Are the materials manageable and usable?

The primary goal of this initial evaluation is to minimize negative impacts and maximize the positive outcomes of the final decision. This process should clarify how to achieve the greatest benefits with the lowest costs and risks. It's realistic to expect that each choice will involve some level of costs, risks, and benefits. However, the key is to determine which option presents the least unfavorable compromises for the school, teachers, and students.

Once the initial cost–risk–benefit analysis is performed, selection of materials should be based on the materials effectiveness. The previous chapters on "Developing STEM Programs" and "Beginning with a Manageable Unit" can provide guidance for reviewing curriculum materials to determine whether they meet student and district needs.

## Considering Different STEM Program Designs

The task of taking action will require an analysis that answers this question: What and where are the greatest opportunities provided by the instructional materials so students will attain the learning outcomes identified? This analysis is based on five aspects of instructional materials. First, the learning

**TABLE 16.1** Preliminary Screen of STEM Materials

| Review Questions | Alignment |
|---|---|
| ♦ Does the unit have a context that lends itself to STEM (e.g., unit is project-based)? | Yes<br>No |
| ♦ Does the unit already include one, two, three, or all four STEM disciplines (i.e., science technology, engineering, or mathematics)? | One<br>Two<br>Three<br>Four |
| ♦ Is the unit based on learning outcomes (e.g., science standards) aligned with STEM disciplines? | Yes<br>No |
| ♦ Are there opportunities to make connections to state standards (e.g., activities have science practices but not engineering)? | Yes<br>No |
| ♦ Do the assessments align with STEM learning outcomes (e.g., summative test is only for science)? | Yes<br>No |

outcomes for the revised unit should be clearly defined. Second, the analysis should consider opportunities to integrate various combinations of the STEM disciplines. Third, the unit analysis should address the dynamics of instruction, including time and opportunities for students to achieve the learning outcomes, with the stipulation that topics and activities must align with these outcomes. Fourth, the unit requires an integrated instructional sequence. Finally, both formative and summative assessments must align with the proposed outcomes and classroom instruction. This preliminary screening is suitable for a small portion of a unit of instruction, such as several lessons. It is advisable to begin with a limited scope—for example, a few lessons within an instructional sequence (see Table 16.1).

The answers to these questions, and those like them, are inherent in the type of STEM program being reviewed.

## Conclusion

This chapter emphasizes that the selection of STEM instructional materials should be a well-informed process. An initial cost–risk–benefit analysis can help guide decision-making, and a thorough evaluation of the materials' effectiveness is crucial to ensure alignment with learning outcomes and STEM education principles.

**Questions for Discussion:**

STEM Educators will Consider:

- Chapters 14, 15, and 16 collectively emphasize the importance of aligning STEM curriculum and instruction with learning goals, research-based practices, and effective evaluation strategies. How can educators and schools create a sustainable process for continuous improvement of their STEM programs, ensuring that they are consistently implementing high-quality, impactful learning experiences for students?
- Considering the guidance provided in these chapters, how can educators effectively advocate for the necessary resources, professional development, and collaborative planning time needed to design and implement rigorous and engaging STEM units that promote deep student understanding and the ability to transfer learning to novel situations?

# 17

# Evaluating STEM Instructional Materials and Resources

Given the importance of selecting appropriate materials for effective STEM instruction important decisions must be made to offer the best resources possible. Educators need to discern which materials best align with their learning goals, instructional practices, and the specific needs of their students. Drawing upon the principles of well-designed STEM units and an understanding of different STEM program designs, this chapter provides a framework for evaluating curriculum resources and materials effectively.

> Aims: To provide STEM educators with a structured approach for evaluating curriculum resources and materials to ensure alignment with effective STEM education principles.
>
> Objectives: Individuals and professional learning teams involved in selecting, adapting, or developing STEM materials will:
>
> - Develop criteria for evaluating STEM curriculum resources based on learning goals, instructional design, and assessment alignment.
> - Understand the strengths and weaknesses of different approaches to STEM integration when evaluating program materials.
> - Consider the practical aspects of implementing resources, including manageability and alignment with current curriculum.

Reflection Questions: STEM educators will consider:

- How well do the materials accommodate the principles of Understanding by Design (UbD) and the development of "Big Ideas" and Transfer Goals?
- Do the materials promote a coherent and purposeful integrated instructional sequence?
- How does the design of the materials reflect different perspectives on STEM integration (e.g., STEM as activity, interdisciplinary, transdisciplinary)?
- Are the materials manageable for classroom implementation, considering the depth, breadth, and interdisciplinary nature of STEM?

Previously we explored several distinct ways in which the acronym STEM is understood and applied in the design of educational programs. Ranging from STEM being used merely as a label for an activity to its implementation as a fully transdisciplinary approach to complex global issues, the chapter highlights the varying levels of integration and clarity in defining the role of science, technology, engineering, and mathematics. Understanding these different perspectives is crucial for educators and curriculum developers as they aim to create meaningful and effective STEM learning experiences.

The models presented offer a framework for considering the advantages and disadvantages of different design specifications, as well as issues related to the scope and sequence of content. Whether STEM is used to denote a collection of related disciplines, a set of overlapping subjects, or a truly integrated program addressing real-world challenges, the clarity of the underlying design significantly impacts the learning outcomes and the students' understanding of the interconnected nature of STEM fields. This foundational understanding of diverse STEM program designs will inform the subsequent discussions in this book. As highlighted in previous chapters, STEM programs can be designed in various ways.

When evaluating resources, consider the underlying design perspective provided in Table 17.1.

## Criteria for Evaluating STEM Resources

Up until this point, we have explored preliminary analysis of curriculum materials to set the stage for a deeper review. The chapter "Beginning with

**TABLE 17.1** Preliminary Screen of STEM Materials

| STEM Conceptualization | Key Characteristics | Evaluation Focus |
|---|---|---|
| STEM as a Slogan/Activity | ◆ Primarily focused on engaging activities.<br>◆ May lack deep disciplinary connections.<br>◆ Might not have a coherent instructional sequence. | ◆ Do the activities genuinely integrate STEM concepts?<br>Or<br>◆ Are they simply science or math activities labeled as STEM? |
| STEM as Disciplines | ◆ Treats STEM as separate subjects taught in coordination.<br>◆ May not provide sufficient opportunities for interdisciplinary problem solving.<br>◆ Might lack the application of knowledge across different STEM fields. | ◆ Are there sufficient opportunities for interdisciplinary problem solving?<br>◆ Can students apply knowledge across different STEM fields effectively? |
| STEM as Interdisciplinary | ◆ Intentionally connects two or more STEM disciplines.<br>◆ Organized around a common theme or project. | ◆ Evaluate the depth and authenticity of the connections between the STEM disciplines. |
| STEM as Transdisciplinary | ◆ Addresses major real-world challenges.<br>◆ Uses the lens of multiple STEM disciplines (and potentially others).<br>◆ Often involves complex scenarios. | ◆ Consider the complexity of the challenges presented.<br>◆ To what extent can students genuinely engage with the interdisciplinary nature of the problem? |

a Manageable STEM Unit" provides guidance on creating STEM units using the Understanding by Design (UbD) framework. It emphasizes the backward design process, starting with desired learning outcomes and aligning assessments and instructional activities accordingly. A key insight from the chapter highlights the importance of focusing on Big Ideas, Transfer Goals, and essential questions to promote deep understanding and the application of learning to new contexts. It also details how to develop coherent instructional sequences, using the 5E model, to facilitate student engagement and the construction of knowledge in a STEM context.

The ideas for unit design can be applied to evaluating commercial programs. For example, to effectively use the provided figure below for evaluating a STEM program, carefully examine the materials in relation to each question. For every criterion, select whether the curriculum fully meets it (Yes), does not meet it (No), or partially meets it (Partially) in the "Evaluation" column. Crucially, support each evaluation with specific examples and observations from the curriculum within the "Notes/Evidence" column to ensure an objective assessment. Finally, always consider your unique teaching context, including your students' needs, available resources, and educational objectives, as you conduct your evaluation.

The first section of the review (see Table 17.2) focuses on how well instructional materials align with established learning goals and relevant STEM

**TABLE 17.2** Evaluation of Alignment with Learning Goals and Standards

| Evaluation Category | Question | Evaluation (Yes/No/Partially) | Notes/Evidence |
|---|---|---|---|
| Alignment with Learning Goals and Standards | ♦ Do the materials clearly articulate learning goals that are relevant and challenging? | | |
| | ♦ How well do the materials align with relevant science, technology, engineering, and mathematics standards? | | Specify the standards being considered (e.g., NGSS, state standards). |
| | ♦ Do the materials emphasize the development of key STEM skills (problem solving, critical thinking, creativity, collaboration)? | | Provide examples of where these skills are emphasized. |

standards. It also examines the extent to which the materials foster the development of crucial STEM skills necessary for student success. These skills, such as problem solving, critical thinking, and collaboration, are fundamental not only for STEM learning but also for broader life applications. Evaluating these aspects is essential to ensure that the chosen resources are purposeful and standards-driven, and contribute to students' overall STEM proficiency.

The following figure outlines criteria related to the instructional design and sequencing of STEM materials. These criteria emphasize the importance of a well-structured pedagogical approach that engages students, promotes active learning, and facilitates the development of deep understanding. A coherent sequence builds upon prior knowledge, gradually increasing in complexity and leading to a culminating learning experience. Evaluating materials using these criteria will help ensure they provide a coherent and effective learning experience.

Effective assessment should not only measure what students have learned but also provide valuable feedback to inform instruction and guide student learning. It is essential to evaluate if the assessments truly align with the intended learning outcomes and instructional activities, ensuring a cohesive and purposeful learning experience. Key considerations include the variety of assessment methods, the demonstration of understanding and application, and opportunities for student reflection and communication. The figure below presents criteria for evaluating assessment alignment in STEM materials (Tables 17.3 and 17.4).

An important aspect of evaluating STEM integration is considering how it aligns with the overall pedagogical goals of the curriculum. For instance, if the goal is to develop students' problem-solving abilities, the materials should provide opportunities for students to apply knowledge and skills from multiple STEM disciplines to solve complex problems. Key considerations include how STEM disciplines are integrated, the authenticity and meaningfulness of the integration, alignment with pedagogical goals, and highlighting connections between STEM fields. Table 17.5. presents criteria for evaluating STEM integration in instructional materials.

Practical considerations such as time constraints, available resources, and the diverse needs of students play a significant role in the successful implementation of any curriculum. When evaluating materials, it is crucial to assess whether they can be realistically adapted and utilized within the specific classroom context. Key considerations include feasibility for implementation,

**TABLE 17.3** Evaluation of Instructional Design and Sequencing

| Evaluation Category | Question | Evaluation (Yes/No/Partially) | Notes/Evidence |
|---|---|---|---|
| Instructional Design and Sequencing | ♦ Do the materials promote an integrated instructional sequence, similar to the 5E model? | | If so, how is this evident in the materials? Are all phases present and well-defined? |
| | ♦ Do the activities and tasks engage students and connect to real-world contexts? | | Describe specific examples of engaging activities and real-world connections. |
| | ♦ Do the materials provide opportunities for hands-on investigation, data collection, and testing of ideas? | | Note the types and frequency of hands-on activities. |
| | ♦ Are there clear pathways for students to articulate evidence-based claims and refine their understanding using STEM terminology? | | How are students supported in developing evidence-based arguments and using precise STEM language? |
| | ♦ Do the materials encourage students to apply learned concepts to new situations and solve problems? | | Provide examples of application activities and problem-solving tasks. |

**TABLE 17.4** Evaluation of Assessment Alignment

| Evaluation Category | Question | Evaluation (Yes/No/Partially) | Notes/Evidence |
|---|---|---|---|
| Assessment Alignment | ♦ Do the materials include a variety of assessment methods aligned with learning goals and activities? | | List the types of assessments included (e.g., formative, summative, performance tasks). |
| | ♦ Do the assessments allow students to demonstrate their understanding and application of STEM concepts and skills? | | How do the assessments go beyond recall of information? |
| | ♦ Are there opportunities for students to reflect on their learning and communicate their findings effectively? | | Describe opportunities for self-reflection and communication of learning. |

**TABLE 17.5** Evaluation of STEM Integration

| Evaluation Category | Question | Evaluation (Yes/No/Partially) | Notes/Evidence |
|---|---|---|---|
| STEM Integration | ♦ How are the STEM disciplines integrated within the materials? | | Describe the nature of the integration (e.g., through projects, activities, thematic units). |
| | ♦ Does the integration feel authentic and meaningful, or is it superficial? | | Explain your reasoning for this assessment. |

*(Continued)*

**TABLE 17.5** (Continued)

| Evaluation Category | Question | Evaluation (Yes/No/Partially) | Notes/Evidence |
|---|---|---|---|
| | ♦ Does the approach to integration align with your pedagogical goals? | | Specify your pedagogical goals related to STEM integration and how the materials align (or don't align). |
| | ♦ Do the materials highlight the connections between different STEM fields? | | Provide examples of explicit connections made between science, technology, engineering, and mathematics. |

**TABLE 17.6** Evaluation of the Manageability and Practicality of STEM Program Integration

| Evaluation Category | Question | Evaluation (Yes/No/Partially) | Notes/Evidence |
|---|---|---|---|
| Manageability and Practicality | ♦ Are the materials feasible for implementation within your classroom context (time, resources, student backgrounds)? | | Consider any limitations or challenges related to time, available materials, technology requirements, and the diverse needs of your students. |
| | ♦ Are the materials clearly organized and user-friendly for both teachers and students? | | Comment on the clarity of instructions, layout, and overall ease of use. |
| | ♦ Do the materials provide adequate support for teachers (background info, guides, rubrics)? | | Describe the types and quality of teacher support materials. |

organization and user-friendliness, and the level of support provided for teachers. Table 17.6 presents criteria for evaluating the manageability and practicality of STEM materials.

## Conclusion

Evaluating STEM curriculum resources and materials is a critical step in providing effective and engaging learning experiences for students. By considering the alignment with learning goals, the quality of instructional design, the integration of assessment, the approach to STEM integration, and the practical aspects of implementation, educators can make informed decisions that lead to meaningful STEM learning. This structured approach will help ensure that chosen resources support the development of essential STEM knowledge, skills, and understandings.

> **Questions for Discussion:**
>
> STEM educators will consider:
>
> ♦ How can the framework for evaluating STEM resources presented in this chapter be adapted or modified to fit the specific needs and constraints of your school or district, including factors such as available resources, student demographics, and local curriculum standards?
> ♦ Considering the different conceptualizations of STEM integration (e.g., STEM as disciplines, interdisciplinary, transdisciplinary), how can educators ensure that the chosen instructional materials foster a deep and meaningful integration of STEM disciplines rather than a superficial or fragmented approach?

# 18

# Curriculum-Based Professional Learning

This chapter's primary themes include practical considerations for high-quality professional STEM learning. Regardless of whether the district and teachers adapt, develop, or select a STEM program, the success of program implementation will largely depend on the professional learning provided for teachers. Recommendations in the chapter synthesize contemporary research on adult learners and effective professional learning environments.

> Aim: To clarify the theme of curriculum-based professional learning and the connections to STEM education.
>
> Purposes: Individuals and professional learning teams considering implementation of STEM programs will:
>
> - Develop a professional learning framework that integrates engagement, analysis, and application, ensuring that educators have the tools to refine their STEM programs effectively, and
> - Bridge research on effective professional learning with instructional practices and strategies.
>
> Reflections: STEM educators will consider:
>
> - What characteristics of professional learning have been most effective in your experience, and how have they influenced your teaching practices?

> How can professional learning be structured to ensure that teachers understand both instructional changes and also feel confident in applying them in their classrooms?

High-quality professional learning creates an experience that is as engaging as it is enlightening. Whether implementing a commercially developed STEM program or a
"homegrown curriculum," teacher leaders should have in-depth experiences with high-quality professional learning. While understanding the Standards is important to professional knowledge, they are already established. The challenge for leaders is using the content of modern standards to promote the innovations needed for implementing STEM with complementary professional learning experiences.

Leaders can look to the research base on the characteristics of effective curriculum-based professional learning that emphasizes the following key features (Linda Darling-Hammond et al., 2017; Short & Hirsh, 2022):

- **Content-focused and standards-aligned**: Deepens educators' understanding of what to teach and how to teach it within the content of the STEM local experiences, and high-quality instructional resources.
- **Equity-focused**: Empower educators to captivate every student, tailoring engaging tasks to diverse needs and abilities.
- **Considerate of adult learners**: Addresses expressed and unexpressed expectations and motivations while attending to mindsets, builds on participants' current knowledge and experience, and invites them to connect learning to meaningful goals and immediate valuable actions.
- **Learner-centric**: Experiences are inquiry-based, interactive, and collaborative. The professional learning experiences involve expert models and practices as educators participate in lessons as learners, plan, internalize, rehearse, observe, and reflect with colleagues who teach in the same content area and use the same instructional program.
- **Provides coaching and expert support**: Offers expertise about the program adopted high-quality instructional resources and evidence-based practices, focused directly on educators' and students' individual needs.

- **Offers feedback and reflection**: Provides job-embedded time for educators to think about intentionally, receive input, and refine practice. Educators need adequate time to learn, rehearse, implement, and reflect upon new strategies that facilitate refinements in practice over time.

## Integrating Inquiry-based Professional Learning for STEM Educators

To foster effective professional learning that aligns with STEM inquiry-based instruction, leaders must create experiences that mirror the active, learning approach required of students (Short & Hirsh, 2022). This approach ensures that teachers understand STEM instructional shifts and experience them firsthand, making the professional learning process more impactful. Following is a step-by-step sequence that supports teachers in engaging, analyzing, and applying STEM learning principles in their classrooms.

## Step 1: Engage Teachers in a STEM Model Lesson as Learners

Begin professional learning with a high-quality STEM model lesson, positioning teachers as proxies for students. By immersing teachers in an authentic inquiry-based experience, they gain firsthand insight into the engagement, exploration, and sensemaking required in STEM instruction. The experiential approach just described allows teachers to better understand the cognitive and instructional demands placed on students, helping them connect STEM content to real-world applications. In addition, this process activates teachers' thinking about content and pedagogy, which will be further developed over time. The importance of priming teacher knowledge cannot be overstated. Having teachers experience the lesson underscores fundamental features of how people learn where current knowledge and experiences catalyze developing new understandings (Bransford, Brown, & Cocking, 2000).

During Step 1, facilitators guide teachers through a series of structured lessons much like those that would occur in a typical school day and desire modern content standards. These lessons are carefully designed to model best practices for STEM programs, demonstrating how inquiry, problem solving, and hands-on exploration can be integrated into instruction. This approach allows teachers to rehearse lessons, fine-tune instructional approaches, and grow more accustomed to the rigor of STEM content. Said differently, Step 1 allows teachers to internalize the rigor of STEM learning and the standards that guide content.

Importantly, this stage emphasizes both content mastery and the development of essential STEM skills—such as critical thinking, collaboration, and persistence—so that teachers can foster these same competencies in their students. For many STEM topics, this may mean developing both content understanding as well as skills and practices for the students. In terms of content, due to the ever-changing nature of STEM knowledge, the theme of the lesson may offer new, different, and deeper content understandings than developed during a teacher's K-16 and other professional experiences. Teachers may have to do hard intellectual work learning content that they have not encountered in their professional preparation. The culmination of these experiences helps shape educators' beliefs about what students can do as a result of high-quality STEM learning and what they can do to facilitate this growth. Step 1 sets the stage for ongoing, content-focused, and learner-centric, all of which are necessary for highly effective curriculum based professional learning (TNTP, 2015) (see Table 18.1).

By participating in hands-on, inquiry-driven learning, teachers develop a deeper appreciation for how students construct understanding—a key step before analyzing instructional design.

For some teachers, their experiences in the STEM model lesson may be different from their past experiences as K-16 STEM students. Other teachers may experience aspects of the model lesson that confirm their beliefs and current practice, but struggle with the issue of making the changes in their instructional design. Regardless, professional learning should view teacher's mindsets as assets for learning. The transition from Steps 1 to 2 in professional

**TABLE 18.1** Key Considerations for Teacher Learning from Model STEM Lessons

| **Key Considerations for Selecting the Model Lesson:** |
| --- |
| ♦ Authenticity & Relevance: Choose a lesson that reflects STEM phenomena or challenges.<br>♦ Interdisciplinary Connections: Ensure the lesson encourages systems thinking and integrates multiple STEM disciplines.<br>♦ Inquiry-Driven: The lesson should focus on problem solving, investigation, and exploration rather than direct instruction. |
| **Teacher Learning Goals During Step 1:** |
| ♦ Experience the intellectual and cognitive demands of STEM learning as students do.<br>♦ Recognize the role of phenomena, problem solving, and data analysis in STEM instruction.<br>♦ Identify how the lesson fosters curiosity, collaboration, and critical thinking. |

learning is critical. Research shows that teachers' mindsets (termed *orientations* in the pedagogical content knowledge literature) can facilitate or constrain their development of professional knowledge (Brown, Friedrichsen, & Abell, 2013; Gess-Newsome, 1999). Taking teachers' mindsets into account helps create a pathway for their growth.

## Step 2: Deconstructing the STEM Learning Experience

Step 2 is all about considering STEM learning from a pedagogical perspective. After engaging in the STEM model lesson, teachers reflect, analyze, and deconstruct their experience using a structured framework. This is where clear instructional design principles and district examples linked to research come in. Step 2 is about helping educators integrate what they know about instructional activities, content, and learners in a very intricate and organized manner. The goal is to connect instructional design principles to effective STEM learning and unpack how the lesson aligns with the goals of high-quality STEM education. We recommend using the major "action-oriented" themes for high-quality instructional design presented earlier in this book that included: (1) Understanding by Design (UbD) and the importance of transfer; (2) effective instructional sequences such as the 5E instructional model; and (3) essential features of meaningful STEM lessons (see Chapters 11, 12, and 14).

Teachers' experience with the model lesson becomes a bridge to developing new understandings about practice. Because there are several proposed considerations, Step 2 may take some time, but the benefits reside in becoming job-embedded practices to reflect on STEM curriculum and instructional design practice. Ultimately, the goal is to begin to develop a new understanding, a powerful type of professional knowledge, achieved through the integration of several instructional considerations (see Table 18.2).

By engaging teachers in this deep-dive analysis, they develop a clearer vision of high-quality STEM instruction, recognizing the importance of inquiry, scaffolding, and evidence-based reasoning in student learning.

## Step 3: Application—Designing and Evaluating STEM Instruction

At Step 3, theory meets practice. Teachers take what they have experienced and analyze it to begin applying their learning by either designing their own STEM units or evaluating current STEM programs (see Table 18.3). This step

**TABLE 18.2** Guiding Questions for Reflection & Analysis

| **1. Unpacking Learning Goals & Transfer** |
|---|
| ♦ What were the big ideas and enduring understandings developed over time?<br>♦ How did the lesson's essential questions drive inquiry and critical thinking?<br>♦ How did the learning experiences support student understanding of STEM-related issues and encourage transfer to new contexts? |
| **2. Sensemaking & Evidence-Based Thinking** |
| ♦ How was participant knowledge activated at the start of the STEM lesson?<br>♦ In what ways did participants have opportunities to collect, analyze, and interpret data?<br>♦ What evidence-based claims could participants construct based on their observations and findings?<br>♦ How did discussions, modeling, or collaboration support meaning-making throughout the lesson? |
| **3. 5E Instructional Model Alignment** |
| ♦ Can participants identify the phases of the 5E Instructional Model (Engage, Explore, Explain, Elaborate, Evaluate) in the lesson?<br>♦ How did each 5E phase build upon the previous one to develop a deeper conceptual understanding?<br>♦ Were there opportunities for students to revise, elaborate, or extend their understanding through hands-on application? |

mirrors the transfer expectations for students in STEM learning—just as students must apply their understanding to new problems, teachers must now apply their professional learning in their specific contexts (Bransford, Brown, & Cocking, 2000). The instructional design principles (from Step 2) are a way of thinking more purposefully and carefully about the nature of *any* design that has the teachers understanding as the goal. Like students, for teachers, active meaning-making refers to the process through which learners construct and derive meaning from their experiences by engaging with authentic tasks and focusing on understanding (Wiggins & McTighe, 2005). Also, like students, teachers must transfer their understanding to meet the needs of their students and unique contexts to develop a deeper conceptual understanding of high-quality STEM instructional design. This is where ongoing coaching and peer-to-peer reflections on practice are key. These assertions are well supported. Hattie's (2023) meta-analysis shows that professional learning is most impactful when teachers have the chance to apply new knowledge to their classrooms and unique contexts and then reflect on their experiences.

**TABLE 18.3** Key Focus Areas for Program Design & Evaluation

| **1. Translating Experience into Unit Planning** |
|---|
| ♦ How can you apply the essential elements of learning, inquiry, and STEM learning to their instruction?<br>♦ What adjustments can be made to existing lessons to strengthen inquiry, problem-solving, and engagement with actual STEM challenges?<br>♦ How can you ensure that their lesson sequences promote knowledge-building over time? |
| **2. Evaluating STEM Program and Practices for Rigor & Alignment** |
| ♦ Does the program intentionally integrate STEM disciplines and reflect standards?<br>♦ Are there opportunities for students to construct meaning through hands-on exploration and investigation?<br>♦ Does the curriculum provide opportunities for students to engage in computational thinking, data analysis, or engineering design? |
| **3. Collaborative Refinement & Implementation** |
| ♦ Provide structured time to collaborate, test ideas, and refine your instructional approaches.<br>♦ Use lesson study cycles, peer feedback, and collaborative planning to refine instructional practices before implementation.<br>♦ Offer ongoing support, coaching, and follow-up to ensure sustainable integration of inquiry-based STEM teaching. |

By completing three steps, teachers begin to gain ownership over their learning, leaving professional learning experiences both with new knowledge, and with practical tools and strategies they can immediately apply to enhance STEM instruction in their classrooms. These assertions align with STEM-specific professional learning research that outlines a cycle of experience, reflection, application and refinement, which is, coincidentally, also similar to how students learning STEM itself (Loucks-Horsley et al., 2010).

## Conclusion

By structuring professional learning to mirror the inquiry-based experiences students engage in, teachers develop a deeper understanding of STEM instructional shifts. This three-step process—experiencing, analyzing, and applying—ensures that teachers internalize the key elements of effective

STEM instruction and gain the confidence to design and implement meaningful learning experiences for their students. Through this iterative and reflective approach, professional learning becomes more than a training session—it transforms into an ongoing process of inquiry, experimentation, and instructional refinement, thereby equipping teachers with the skills to cultivate a culture of STEM inquiry in their classrooms.

**Questions for Discussion:**

STEM educators will consider:

- The chapter outlines a three-step process for curriculum-based professional learning: Engage, Analyze, and Apply. How can schools and districts structure professional learning experiences to ensure that teachers have sufficient time and support to move through each of these steps effectively, ultimately leading to sustainable changes in classroom practice?
- Effective STEM professional learning should be "learner-centric," mirroring the inquiry-based and collaborative nature of STEM instruction itself. What are some practical strategies for incorporating active learning, reflection, and peer feedback into professional learning experiences to model these essential elements of STEM pedagogy?

## References

Bransford, J., Brown, A., & Cocking, R. (2000). *How People Learn: Brain, Mind, Experience, and School*. Washington, DC: National Academies Press.

Brown, P., Friedrichsen, P., & Abell, S. (2013). The development of prospective secondary biology teachers, pedagogical content knowledge (PCK). *The Journal of Science Teacher Education*, Vol. 24(1): pp. 133–155.

Darling-Hammond, L., Hyler, M. E., & Gardner, M. (2017). *Effective Teacher Professional Development*. Palo Alto, CA: Learning Policy Institute.

Gess-Newsome, J. (1999). PCK: An introduction and orientation. In Gess-Newsome, J. & Lederman, N. (Eds.), *Examining PCK: The Construct and its Implications for Science Education* (pp. 3–20). Netherlands: Kluwer Academic Publishers.

Hattie, J. (2023). *Visible Learning: The Sequel: A Synthesis of Over 2,100 Meta-Analyses Relating to Achievement* (1st ed.). New York and London: Routledge Publishing. https://doi.org/10.4324/9781003380542

Loucks-Horsley, S., Stiles, K. E., Mundry, S., Love, N., & Hewson, P. W. (2010). *Designing Professional Development for Teachers of Science and Mathematics* (3rd ed.). Thousand Oaks, CA: Corwin Press.

Short, J. B., & Hirsh, S. (2022). *Transforming Teaching Through Curriculum-based Professional Learning: The Elements*. Thousand Oaks, CA: Corwin Press.

The New Teacher Project (TNTP). (2015). *The Mirage: Confronting the Hard Truth About Our Quest for Teacher Development*. New York: TNTP. https://tntp.org/assets/documents/TNTP-Mirage_2015.pdf

Wiggins, G., & McTighe, J. (2005). *Understanding by Design* (Expanded 2nd ed.). Alexandria, VA: ASCD.

# 19

# Our Vision for Your Guidance and Leadership in STEM Education

This chapter begins with a brief review of the book's themes and a vision for STEM in American education. The chapter continues with discussions of leadership roles and guides.

> Aim: To clarify the possible roles for guidance and leadership in STEM education.
>
> Objectives: Individuals assuming leadership and initiating reforms for STEM programs and practices will:
>
> ♦ Gain useful options about leadership roles,
> ♦ Acquire knowledge about fundamentals of effective leadership, and
> ♦ Review priorities for leadership strategies.
>
> Reflection:
>
> ♦ The book's chapters are structured to progress from discussions of current STEM realities and possibilities to descriptions of disciplines and concrete recommendations for instructional materials. How has this specific sequence of topics deepened your understanding of

> STEM education, and in what ways might this progression inform your own efforts to plan or implement STEM initiatives?
> 
> ♦ The book aims to establish STEM as a crucial innovation by helping educational leaders understand the disciplines, connecting purposes and policies to programs, clarifying effective teaching practices, and recognizing STEM's contributions to societal challenges. Reflect on which of these aims you found most impactful for your professional role, and how the book has specifically equipped you to pursue that aim.

## Are You Ready to Provide Guidance and to Lead?

Are you willing and ready to assume the responsibilities of leadership? If you have a positive response, a reasonable first question may be—"Where do I begin?" You can begin with a review and introspection of your goals, aspirations, opportunities and understanding of rewards and problems associated with leadership.

The second question is, "Whom am I leading?" Obviously, you may have initial answers—your students, the science teachers in your district or state, your colleagues in STEM education, your community, and so on. However, there is another answer that may be more subtle and elusive. We refer to the motives, needs, aspirations, and goals of potential followers, as individuals and as groups. There should be some congruence between your motives and goals and those of your followers. Leadership will probably be a combination of the transactional and transformational, but you should base it on an accurate view of your followers' motives and goals.

Work on this book includes reviewing ideas about effective leadership. Guiding principles are from the original work of Steven R. Covey books (1989, 1992), will be quite helpful. Table 19.1 lists the *Seven Habits of Highly Effective People* that Covey made popular.

**TABLE 19.1** Seven Habits of Highly Effective People and Principle-Based Leadership

| |
|---|
| 1. Be proactive |
| 2. Begin with the end in mind |
| 3. Put first things first |
| 4. Think win–win |
| 5. Seek first to understand, then to be understood |
| 6. Synergize |
| 7. Sharpen the Saw |

Although Covey's discussions range from deeply personal to highly philosophical, we think several of the habits represent reasonable and helpful guiding principles. For example, "Begin with the end in mind" can easily be associated with a leaders' need to have a vision. One should imagine the consequences of implementing science standards and advancing STEM education. Being able to imagine change and anchor a presentation in the science standards will be immensely helpful. The logical extension of beginning with the end is planning a course of action to achieve the change.

Another habit that will certainly advance your ability to lead is "Seek first to understand, the to be understood." All of us want to be understood, that includes both you and those who you are leading. Teachers who have to change have concerns (e.g., What do you mean by STEM education? What do these new standards mean for my teaching?) that may dominate their ability to listen. Here is a strategy we have found effective. Begin a presentation with a statement such as: "My discussion today is about STEM education and the new Standards for science." Before my presentation, I would like to hear about your concerns." An extension of this habit is to plan for and be able to answer questions such as: "What does the science practice of formulating an evidence-based argument mean for third grade?" Or "Will the science content prepare students for college, careers, and citizenship?"

Contemporary justification for a vision of improved STEM education may reside in themes such as "economic stability," "basic skills for the 21st century workforce," and "resource use and environmental quality." Such themes differ from earlier justifications such as the "space race" and "a nation at risk." The economic rationale emerged from a significant recession, the realization that the U.S. economy is part of a global economy, and that the current administration's policies influence the rate and direction of a country's economic progress. The themes of resource use and environmental quality relate to the economic theme and issues such as climate change.

Concretely, contemporary vision resides in national and state standards and the implied reform of curriculum, instruction, and assessments. Providing leadership requires communicating a vision for those who wish to lead. To state the obvious, the vision need not be complex and complicated; but it must be different from the status quo. The vision must be new, substantial, and look to the future. The title *Science for All Americans* (Rutherford & Ahlgren, 1989) is an excellent example of a vision from recent history. In this era, the *Next Generation Science Standards, For States, By States* NGSS Lead States, 2013) expresses a vision and locates the importance of states in the reform.

Communicating the vision requires a translation from the abstract, for example of the latter is translating state policies to school programs and teaching practices at the local level.

All of this said, leaders have to recognize the power of the past may be a force against a new vision. Those in the community will evaluate the leaders' vision with their vision grounded in the past or current situation. We cannot say what the evaluation will entail; but we can guarantee that it will be grounded in the past. "Where is my topic in the new standards?," "Will teaching scientific practices be on the state test?" Being able to illustrate the vision with examples that constituents recognize will be most helpful.

A complement to vision is a plan. Expressing a new vision for STEM education is one thing. It is quite another to provide a plan for achieving that vision. The plan must have clear and concrete examples for constituents. A vision of STEM is okay; but what does it mean for school programs in general and my classroom practices in particular?

So, leadership requires both a vision and a plan. If one only has a vision, you are like a utopian thinker. A utopian thinker encompasses the mental act of envisioning an ideal society. If you only have a plan, your likely are a manager, not a leader.

Among the essentials of leadership, we would list the importance of a leader's ability to recognize and address the political realities of his or her work. Our first insight here is that the leader has to recognize that initiating changes means addressing the politics. Not all issues are solely educational. Indeed, it may be the case that all educational issues ultimately may be political. A paradox imbedded here can be stated as achieving educational goals while addressing political realities. We have found that *either/or* thinking often expresses the paradox, while *both/and* thinking provides insights into the resolutions.

Experience teaches one more lesson for those in leadership positions. If you are leading, you cannot avoid conflict and controversy. And the larger the system and greater the change, the more controversy you will experience. Indeed, this is another paradox. It can be thought of as—achieving your goals requires enduring criticism. And, unfortunately, the criticism is often unfair, constant, and personal.

What lessons have we learned that might guide readers in their careers? We divide this discussion into two categories. First, there are several general ideas of leadership. Second, there are specific ideas related to programs and practices.

Concerning leadership in STEM education, our first suggestion is "be a leader;" do not wait for others to show the way. As opportunities for leadership emerge, for example, new standards for science education and need for changing the school science program become involved. Learn about the standards and develop an understanding of what the new standards may mean for your state, district, or school.

Your leadership should include both a vision and a plan or strategies for change. We underscore the need for *both* a vision and a plan. If an individual has only a vision, there may be excitement and support, but the changes will flounder—and likely fail—based on questions of "What do we do?," "What should change?," "What does this mean for me and my students?" On the other hand, having only a plan encounters problems with questions such as "Why are we doing this?," "How does this change relate to others at the national, state, or district level?" The effective leader must have answers to questions such as these.

Here are several insights we have learned about leadership and reform of school programs and teaching practices. These may seem like contradictions, but the effective leader is able to resolve them. The context of this discussion is the reform initiated by *A Framework for K-12 Science Education* (NRC, 2012) and the *Next Generation Science Standards* (NGSS Lead States, 2013). Our reference to new standards may be the national, state, or local standards.

Individuals will ask for more information about the new standards: yet they will report inadequacies and concerns about the standards. Take the expression of concerns seriously. The individuals, often teachers, are the ones confronted with significant change, and they may rightfully express concerns.

Another paradox of leadership is the need to fulfill a national or state agenda and respond to local requirements. This requires attention to recognizing the local mandates and addressing them in the translation of policies (i.e., standards) to school programs and classroom practice.

While it is true that the new standards are abstract and general policies, leadership requires acting concretely. You should recognize the role and goal of new standards and be able to describe changes in school programs and classroom practices at elementary, middle, and high school levels.

By the very nature of implementing new standards, you are initiating change in the educational system. The other part of the paradox is maintaining continuity in various components of the system. For example, the changes may be to the content emphasis and organization, but there is still life, Earth, and physical sciences.

To conclude, leadership matters in STEM education and requires us to acknowledge, live with, and resolve paradoxes. Often the politics and realities of education reduce our aspirations. This should not deter your leadership in general, or recognizing the role of purposes, policies programs, and practices in particular. It will be the students as future citizens who benefit from your leadership.

## References

Covey, S. R. (1989). *The 7 Habits of Highly Effective People*. New York: Simon & Schuster.

Covey, S. R. (1992). *Principle-Centered Leadership*. New York: Simon & Schuster.

National Research Council (NRC). (2012). *A Framework for K-12 Science Education: Practices, Crosscutting Concepts, and Core Ideas*. Washington, DC: The Nation Academies Press.

NGSS/Lead States. (2013). *Next Generation Science Standards for States, By States*. Washington, DC: The National Academies Press.

Rutherford, J., & Ahlgren, A., (1989). *Science for All Americans*. New York: Oxford University Press.

For Product Safety Concerns and Information please contact our EU representative GPSR@taylorandfrancis.com
Taylor & Francis Verlag GmbH, Kaufingerstraße 24, 80331 München, Germany

www.ingramcontent.com/pod-product-compliance
Lightning Source LLC
Chambersburg PA
CBHW060315240426
43661CB00059B/2768